THE SOVIET MILITARY
AND U.S. DEFENSE PLANNING

STUDIES IN DEFENSE POLICY

THE SOVIET MILITARY BUILDUP AND U.S. DEFENSE SPENDING

Barry M. Blechman

Robert P. Berman

Martin Binkin

Stuart E. Johnson

Robert G. Weinland

Frederick W. Young

THE BROOKINGS INSTITUTION

Washington, D.C.

Library of Congress Cataloging in Publication data:

Main entry under title:

The Soviet military buildup and U.S. defense spending.

   (Studies in defense policy)
   First published in the 1977 ed. of Setting national
priorities.
   Includes bibliographical references.
   1. United States—Defenses.   2. United States—
Armed Forces—Appropriations and expenditures.
3. Russia—Defenses.   4. Russia—Armed Forces—
Appropriations and expenditures.   I. Blechman, Barry M.
II. Series.
UA23.S55   355.03'3004'7   77-86492
ISBN 0-8157-0989-7

9 8 7 6 5 4 3 2 1

THE BROOKINGS INSTITUTION is an independent organization devoted to nonpartisan research, education, and publication in economics, government, foreign policy, and the social sciences generally. Its principal purposes are to aid in the development of sound public policies and to promote public understanding of issues of national importance.

The Institution was founded on December 8, 1927, to merge the activities of the Institute for Government Research, founded in 1916, the Institute of Economics, founded in 1922, and the Robert Brookings Graduate School of Economics and Government, founded in 1924.

The Board of Trustees is responsible for the general administration of the Institution, while the immediate direction of the policies, program, and staff is vested in the President, assisted by an advisory committee of the officers and staff. The by-laws of the Institution state: "It is the function of the Trustees to make possible the conduct of scientific research, and publication, under the most favorable conditions, and to safeguard the independence of the research staff in the pursuit of their studies and in the publication of the results of such studies. It is not a part of their function to determine, control, or influence the conduct of particular investigations or the conclusions reached."

The President bears final responsibility for the decision to publish a manuscript as a Brookings book. In reaching his judgment on the competence, accuracy, and objectivity of each study, the President is advised by the director of the appropriate research program and weighs the views of a panel of expert outside readers who report to him in confidence on the quality of the work. Publication of a work signifies that it is deemed a competent treatment worthy of public consideration but does not imply endorsement of conclusions or recommendations.

The Institution maintains its position of neutrality on issues of public policy in order to safeguard the intellectual freedom of the staff. Hence interpretations or conclusions in Brookings publications should be understood to be solely those of the authors and should not be attributed to the Institution, to its trustees, officers, or other staff members, or to the organizations that support its research.

FOREWORD

The Soviet Union has been strengthening its military capabilities for more than twelve years. Although there seems to have been no sudden spurt in Soviet defense programs, gradual and sustained improvements across the full range of military forces have significantly altered their size, structure, and technological sophistication.

Concern over the implications of these changes has led to renewed emphasis among Western nations on requirements for an adequate defense. In particular, perceptions of a growing military threat from the USSR were a major factor in reversing the 1968–75 decline in real expenditures by the U.S. Department of Defense.

The authors of this study argue that an effective response by the United States requires an understanding of the specific nature of the threats posed by the Soviet buildup. If the needs of defense are to be met effectively and at reasonable cost, priorities must be established and resources allocated accordingly.

To promote such an understanding, the authors review shifts in the balance of conventional military power in Europe, the Middle East, and East Asia, and evaluate trends in the strategic nuclear balance. With the perspective provided by their analysis they examine the U.S. defense program and advocate changes they regard as desirable.

This study—the seventeenth in the Brookings series of Studies in Defense Policy—was first published in July 1977 as the fourth chapter in the Brookings book, *Setting National Priorities: The 1978 Budget*, edited by Joseph A. Pechman. The text has been revised to reflect recent developments, of which the most important was the cancellation of the B-1 bomber program.

Barry M. Blechman is the head of the Brookings defense analysis staff, of which his coauthors were members at the time this study was prepared. All six authors are grateful to John Baker, Penelope Harpold, and Christine Lipsey for ensuring the accuracy of the data presented, to Elizabeth H. Cross for editing the manuscript, to Robert W. Hartman, and Joseph A. Pechman for their comments, and to Georgiana S. Hernandez, who bore the secretarial burdens with her usual good spirit. They are especially indebted to Edward R. Fried, who guided the project at the beginning and provided useful advice at every stage.

The Institution gratefully acknowledges the assistance of the Ford Foundation, whose grant helps to support its work in defense studies. The views expressed here are those of the authors alone, and should not be ascribed to the Ford Foundation, or to the trustees, officers, or other staff members of the Brookings Institution.

BRUCE K. MACLAURY
President

July 1977
Washington, D.C.

THE SOVIET MILITARY BUILDUP
AND U.S. DEFENSE SPENDING

Barry M. Blechman

Robert P. Berman

Martin Binkin

Stuart E. Johnson

Robert G. Weinland

Frederick W. Young

IN FISCAL YEAR 1978 the U.S. defense budget will again increase substantially, the result of planning decisions taken three years ago. At that time, the Ford administration argued that the decline in defense spending and military force levels since 1968 had gone about as far as it could without endangering the nation's security. Consequently, larger defense appropriations were requested to increase the number of Army divisions, Navy ships, and Air Force tactical aircraft wings, accelerate the modernization of both strategic and conventional weapon systems, and improve the readiness of military units for combat. In the face of a growing Soviet military threat, administration spokesmen stated, a sustained defense buildup was necessary to assure U.S. security "over the long-haul." Even on the assumption that substantial savings would be realized by more efficient management of defense resources, this meant a steady rise in spending in real terms (i.e., after allowing for inflation) well into the future. Although Congress refused to authorize real growth in defense obligations in fiscal 1975, it did approve the principal elements of the Ford program, making future increases inevitable. The defense budget has risen each year since.

The importance of fiscal 1975 as a turning point in U.S. defense

1

Table 1. Trend of the Defense Budget, Current and Constant Fiscal 1978 Dollars, Selected Fiscal Years, 1964–82

Component	1964	1968	1975	1977	1978[a]	1982[b]
Total obligational authority						
(billions of current dollars)	**50.6**	**75.6**	**87.8**	**110.2**	**120.4**	**166.8**
Baseline forces	48.4	53.6	79.2	100.9	110.3	153.7
Retired pay	1.2	2.1	6.2	8.2	9.1	12.1
Military assistance	1.0	0.6	1.6	1.1	1.0	1.0
Cost of Vietnam War	...	19.3	0.9	...	...	...
Total outlays (billions of						
current dollars)	**50.8**	**78.0**	**86.0**	**98.3**	**110.1**	**156.4**
Total obligational authority						
(billions of 1978 dollars)	**124.7**	**154.7**	**106.6**	**116.9**	**120.4**	**138.6**
Baseline forces	119.5	113.3	95.7	107.1	110.3	128.0
Retired pay	3.1	4.6	7.8	8.7	9.1	9.8
Military assistance	2.1	1.1	1.9	1.1	1.0	0.8
Cost of Vietnam War	...	37.7	1.2	...	...	...
Total outlays (billions of 1978						
dollars)	**123.2**	**158.3**	**105.0**	**104.6**	**109.7**	**129.2**
Total defense outlays as a						
percentage of						
GNP	8.2	9.4	5.9	5.5	5.6	5.4
Federal budget outlays	42.9	43.6	26.4	23.9	25.0	28.0

Sources: 1964–77, from data provided by the Department of Defense, 1977; 1978 budget from Department of Defense, "Annual Defense Department Report, FY 1978" (January 17, 1977; processed), and "FY 1978 Amended Department of Defense Budget," news release 72-77 (February 22, 1977); 1982 projections from Department of Defense, "FY 1978 Department of Defense Budget," news release 17-77 (January 17, 1977). Figures are rounded.
   a. As proposed by the Ford administration and amended by President Carter.
   b. As projected by the Ford administration.

policy is reflected in the budgetary data shown in table 1. By then, as measured in constant dollars, defense expenditures had declined by one-third from the Vietnam War peak. This decline proved to be an important source for financing both domestic programs and tax reductions. Actually, the reduction in defense spending amounted to more than a dismantling of the additional forces that had been created to fight the war. If the effects of inflation are discounted, the fiscal 1975 cost of baseline forces (excluding retired pay, military assistance, and residual Vietnam War expenses) was about one-fifth lower than in fiscal 1964, the last pre-Vietnam peacetime budget. From 1964 levels, military manpower in 1975 was down by one-fifth, the number of Navy ships by close to one-half, and the number of strategic defensive forces by more than two-thirds.

The defense buildup that began three years ago is reversing these

**Table 2. Changes in Total Obligational Authority for Baseline Forces
between Fiscal Years 1975 and 1978**
Billions of fiscal 1978 dollars

Component	Change
Procurement	13.8
Purchases for operations and maintenance	3.3
Research and development	1.7
Pay and related items	−1.7
Military construction	−0.6
Total	16.5

Source: Authors' estimates derived from data provided by the Office of the Assistant Secretary of Defense, (Comptroller), March 1977.

trends. For fiscal 1978 President Ford requested authority to obligate $123 billion for national defense; $13 billion more than the previous year, or an increase of $7 billion (6 percent) allowing for inflation. Further annual real increases of 3 percent were projected for fiscal 1979 through 1982. The Ford 1978 defense budget would have shown real growth of $16.5 billion, or 16 percent, from fiscal 1975, most of which would have been earmarked for investment—to procure new military hardware and to expand research and development. The cost of defense manpower, a rising expense in the first half of the 1970s, has actually declined slightly during the past three years (table 2). As shown in table 3, the five categories of combat forces have shared this increase in procurement funds in rough proportion to their share of the total budget, except for a relative increase in the amount allocated to tactical air forces at the expense of ground combat forces.

President Carter's amendments to the 1978 budget would not change this picture much. His proposals would reduce total obligational authority for defense by $2.8 billion and outlays by $400 million. Some weapon programs would be terminated (e.g., the nuclear strike cruiser, the A-7 aircraft, and the nonnuclear version of the LANCE missile); for others, the number to be purchased in fiscal 1978 would be cut back (e.g., attack submarines and F-15 fighters); and the decision to go ahead with some programs would be deferred (e.g., procurement of a new tanker-cargo aircraft and full-scale development of the M-X missile). Although these changes may signal important future shifts in defense priorities, in themselves they neither constitute a clear departure in force planning nor necessarily presage

Table 3. Distribution of the Increase in Procurement Authorizations between Fiscal Years 1975 and 1978
Amounts in billions of fiscal 1978 dollars

	Increase in procurement funds, 1975–78		Type of force as a percentage of baseline budget, 1975
Type of force	*Amount*	*Percentage of total*	
Tactical air[a]	4.4	32	25
Ground combat[b]	3.6	26	31
Strategic[c]	2.8	20	21
Naval[d]	2.7	20	20
Mobility	0.3	2	3
Total	13.8	100	100

Sources: Authors' estimates derived from data appearing in *The Budget of the United States Government—Appendix*, fiscal years 1975–78; Department of Defense, "Program Acquisition Costs by Weapon System, Department of Defense Budget for Fiscal Year 1975," and for fiscal years 1976, 1977, and 1978. Each type of combat force's share of the total baseline budget is calculated by the methodology used in chapter 8 of Edward R. Fried and others, *Setting National Priorities: The 1974 Budget* (Brookings, 1973), in which all support costs, direct and indirect, are allocated to combat forces.

a. One-half of the increase would be used for procurement of Air Force fighter-attack aircraft; the remainder for support equipment, ordnance, and electronic warfare. Navy aircraft procurement remained roughly constant in real terms.

b. The proposed increase would be spread among hundreds of items. Total tank acquisition (M-48, M-60, and XM-1) would show net real growth of about $0.4 billion; Marine Corps equipment purchases would rise by $0.2 billion.

c. Increase accounted for by strategic submarine and missile programs and manned bombers and their armament. These rises would be offset somewhat by decreased spending for land-based missiles.

d. Spending for nuclear-powered submarines and surface ships would remain roughly constant; the increase would be used mainly for conventionally powered escorts.

future reductions in military spending. In effect, the new administration has not yet articulated the direction of its defense planning.[1]

For present purposes, therefore, it can be assumed that, as outlined in President Ford's budget, defense expenditures are likely to (1) rise at about the same rate as the gross national product, declining only slightly to 5.4 percent of the nation's resources; and (2) absorb a moderately rising proportion of the total federal budget, growing from the present 25 percent to about 28 percent over the next five years. In relative terms, this budgetary prospect is by no means alarming; the proportionate burden of defense will remain substantially lower than it was ten or fifteen years ago. Nonetheless, budgetary resources will continue to be scarce in the years ahead. Hence, the fact that the level of defense expenditures is already large in absolute

1. In general, compared to the Ford defense program, the Carter budget amendments indicate less emphasis on strategic nuclear forces, a more stringent review of the need for high-cost weapon systems, greater emphasis on strengthening U.S. military capabilities in Europe, and a shift away from nuclear-powered surface warships. The significance of these changes for future defense costs cannot be determined, however, until next year's budget, which the Carter administration alone will shape.

terms and will rise further in the future poses difficult questions about how the requirements of national security should be met and about how those requirements compare with competing national priorities.

In seeking reasons for the continuing buildup of U.S. military capabilities, we should look to the political scene abroad, which has in some respects improved recently but still remains dangerous.

Both the Syrian and the Egyptian governments appear to have adopted a more moderate approach to the issues concerning Israel and the Palestinians. There seems at least a chance that negotiations between Israel and its neighbors will begin this year. Moreover, the Soviet position in the Middle East has continued to erode both politically and militarily. Consequently, for the next year or so, the likelihood of a new Arab-Israeli conflict with its attendant risk of U.S. military involvement seems low.

In China, the uncertainty about who would succeed Mao has been resolved, and a pragmatic leadership seemingly committed to continuing rapprochement with the United States has come to power. Elsewhere in East Asia, fears that the U.S. defeat in Indochina would result in new fighting in Southeast Asia or in a more aggressive stance by the North Koreans appear to have been ill founded. For the present, at least, political relations in East Asia are relatively calm.

On the other hand, Soviet policy has not changed. The USSR clearly is willing to use force, or to support the use of force by others, to exploit opportunities for expanding its influence in the third world. The tough stance adopted by communist officials against dissidents in the USSR, East Germany, and Czechoslovakia and renewed pressure on Yugoslavia show that Soviet leaders are determined to maintain their control of Eastern Europe. And the buildup of Soviet armed forces continues without apparent letup.

A sober judgment thus would be that the risk of U.S.-Soviet armed confrontation remains what it has been for many years: low though not negligible. Although it has been possible to reach some arms control agreements with the Russians and the East-West political situation in Europe has been stabilized, U.S.-Soviet relations are still the uneasy mixture of cooperation and competition that has marked them throughout the postwar period. In judging the risk of conflict, however, one must concentrate on the conflicts within specific countries or regions that could bring the superpowers into collision.

Although there has been some improvement in the Middle East, the gap between the Arab and Israeli terms for peace remains wide. If progress toward resolution of these differences remains elusive, the dynamics of Arab politics will make it difficult to avoid hostilities once Egyptian and Syrian military capabilities have been strengthened sufficiently. In the event of a new war, the possibility of Soviet intervention could not be precluded. If that occurred, only U.S. counteraction could restore the balance.

The results of continuing tension between Eastern European nationalism and Soviet domination are hard to predict. There are special risks in Yugoslavia, where post-Tito internal conflict could lead to Soviet intervention, which, if it did not succeed quickly, could lead to wider conflict.

In Korea, two hostile and seemingly unpredictable regimes confront each other. Conflict is deterred by the existence of a rough balance of military power on the peninsula and the restraints imposed by the major powers. If that balance should change—through expansion on one side and decline on the other or through internal disruption in one of the Korean states—conflict could ensue. Neither the United States nor the USSR could in such a circumstance readily countenance the destruction of its ally.

Admittedly the risks of such confrontations are small. A succession of Arab-Israeli wars has failed to involve U.S. and Soviet military forces in armed conflict. The likelihood of Soviet intervention and Western counterintervention in Yugoslavia is low. The likelihood of large-scale aggression in Korea is slight. Still, the risks are there and, taken together, they are not trivial. And even where there now appears to be virtually no risk of conflict—notably in Central Europe—most observers agree that the maintenance of a stable and visible balance of military power is essential to prevent adverse political developments.

None of this is new. But one factor has changed: the quality and quantity of military power that the Soviet Union can bring to bear in support of its political objectives around the world. It is this worrisome evolution of Soviet military capabilities that has provided the main impetus for a rising U.S. defense budget and the receptive attitude toward higher defense appropriations of Congress and the public.

Developments in Soviet Military Capabilities*

In dollar terms, Soviet defense outlays for 1976 are estimated to have been $120 billion, about one-third more than those of the United States.[2] This estimate is derived by assessing the size of the Soviet defense effort in some detail, and costing each operational unit, procurement program, and so forth, at U.S. prices. This methodology has its drawbacks. For instance, measuring the Soviet defense budget in U.S. defense prices means that the high pay scales of a volunteer army are applied to the large conscripted force of the Soviet Union. This is illogical because if the USSR had to pay American wages to its military personnel it probably would not maintain so large a standing force. The CIA also measures the Soviet defense budget in rubles, but this too causes problems—principally because the ruble price of many items of military hardware can only be approximated very roughly. Still, so long as common assumptions are applied, comparisons of annual data on Soviet defense spending, expressed in either rubles or dollars, can indicate important trends.

Since the mid-1960s, these data reveal steady growth in the Soviet defense budget, averaging about 3 percent annually when expressed in constant U.S. prices, and around 5 percent annually when expressed in rubles. This suggests a cumulative increase over the period of between 40 and 70 percent. These aggregate figures, however, cloak important distinctions in the relative emphasis placed on different types of forces; they are best examined individually.

Strategic Nuclear Forces

Soviet leaders accord high priority to the strategic rocket forces. Since 1964 Soviet aggregate strategic nuclear capabilities have increased roughly fivefold (see table 4). Improvements have been made steadily and continue to be made.

At present, three new types of intercontinental ballistic missiles (ICBMs) are being deployed, deployment of a fourth is expected shortly, and two new types of submarine-launched ballistic missiles (SLBMs) have been flight-tested. Four of the six can be equipped with multiple independently targetable reentry vehicles (MIRVs);

* This section was prepared by Robert P. Berman.
2. U.S. Central Intelligence Agency, "A Dollar Cost Comparison of Soviet and U.S. Defense Activities, 1966–1976," SR 77-10001U (January 1977; processed).

Table 4. Soviet Strategic Forces, 1964, 1970, and 1976

Description	1964[a]	1970	1976
Force levels (launchers)	473	1,685	2,498
ICBMs	190	1,287	1,567
SLBMs	108	254	791
Heavy bombers (long range)	175	145	140
Throw-weight (millions of pounds)[b]	2.2	6.6	9.6
Missiles only	0.8	5.5	8.6
Targetable warheads (missile reentry vehicles and bombs)[c]	649	1,832	3,228
Missiles only	298	1,541	2,948
Equivalent megatonnage[d]	1,102	3,396	4,861
Missiles only	534	2,923	4,406

Sources: Authors' estimates derived from International Institute for Strategic Studies, *The Military Balance, 1976–1977* (London: IISS, 1976), pp. 8, 73–75; Stockholm International Peace Research Institute, *World Armaments and Disarmament: SIPRI Yearbook 1976* (M.I.T. Press, 1976), pp. 24–27; "Annual Defense Department Report, FY 1978," p. 58; and declassified posture statements of the Secretaries of Defense to the U.S. Congress, Fiscal Years 1963–73 (processed).

a. Figures for 1964 include *Golf*-class and *Zulu*-class ballistic missile submarines.

b. The weight-carrying capacity of missiles and bombers is not directly comparable. This index includes the payload of each system that could be used to carry nuclear weapons, its protective structure, and associated guidance system.

c. Targetable warheads include only weapons associated with on-line forces.

d. Equivalent megatonnage is a measure of the area destruction capacity of a nuclear arsenal based on the number and explosive yields of its various component weapons and the fact that the extent of the ground area that would be destroyed by a nuclear explosion does not increase one-to-one with increases in the yield of the nuclear warhead.

all incorporate significant improvements in accuracy. Six additional intercontinental missile systems are said to be in earlier stages of development and may be operational in the 1980s.

Soviet strategic air defenses also are being modernized, despite declining budgetary emphasis on this function. Although the number of interceptor aircraft in PVO Strany, the USSR's air defense command, has dropped by about one-third since 1964, the force's total capabilities are probably greater now because of the introduction of advanced surface-to-air missiles, aircraft, and radars.

Other developments in Soviet military capabilities have also raised concern among some American observers because of their possible implications for the outcome of strategic nuclear conflicts.

• A new medium-range bomber, Backfire, and a new intermediate-range ballistic missile, SS-20, are being deployed. Although both systems appear to be primarily designed for use in Europe or against China, they could be used against the United States. The Backfire could reach targets in the continental United States if refueled during flight, staged through Arctic bases, or recovered in third nations (e.g.,

Cuba). The SS-20 apparently uses the same transporter and the first two stages of a new Soviet ICBM. Some American analysts believe that as a consequence deployed SS-20s could be converted rapidly for intercontinental use.

• Since 1971, Soviet civil defense efforts seem to have intensified. These include the construction of hardened command-and-control centers and storage sites for various critical items, the preparation of city evacuation plans, and possibly measures to protect essential industrial plants from nuclear attack.

• Finally, the Soviet Union has been experimenting with techniques to destroy satellites. An attack on U.S. early warning and other intelligence and communications satellites would probably be the first step in any sizable nuclear exchange.

Although the individual significance of each of these measures is a matter of some controversy, the sheer scope and momentum of the Soviet strategic program is not, and has caused widespread concern in the United States.

Ground Forces

The ground forces dominate the Soviet defense establishment. From 1964 to 1976 Soviet ground forces expanded from 140 divisions to 170, an increase of 21 percent, and were extensively redeployed. The largest increase took place in the Far East, where approximately 29 divisions have been sent since 1964. The number of Soviet divisions deployed in Eastern Europe was increased from 26 to 31 when one of the army groups that occupied Czechoslovakia in 1968 remained there. In the western Soviet Union, where the immediate strategic reserve for war in Europe is located, the number of divisions increased from 60 to 64.

Changes in the structure of Soviet ground forces are summarized in table 5. Although the greatest growth in divisions occurred in the Far East, one-half of the Soviet Army is clearly positioned for war in Europe. There are other indications of this priority. New types of equipment for the ground forces, for example, are usually deployed first to Soviet forces in Eastern Europe, particularly to the Group of Soviet Forces Germany. Indeed, the size of each of the 20 divisions that now make up the GSFG has been increased, with a better than 20 percent rise in the manpower assigned to each, a 40 percent increase in the number of tanks in each of the 10 motorized rifle divi-

Table 5. Changes in Soviet Ground Forces, by Type and Location, 1964 and 1976
Number of divisions

Type	Eastern Europe		Western USSR		Far East		Central and southern USSR	
	1964	*1976*	*1964*	*1976*	*1964*	*1976*	*1964*	*1976*
Armored	13	14	20	23	3	7	14	4
Motorized	13	17	34	35	13	38	23	25
Airborne	0	0	6	6	1	1	0	0
Total[a]	26	31	60	64	17	46	37	29

Sources: Authors' estimates derived from data appearing in IISS, *The Military Balance, 1964–1965* (London: IISS, 1964); IISS, *The Military Balance, 1976–1977; Fiscal Year 1978 Authorization for Military Procurement, Research and Development, and Active Duty, Selected Reserve, and Civilian Personnel Strengths*, Hearings before the Senate Armed Services Committee, 95:1 (GPO, 1977), pt. 2, p. 1155; and Department of the Army, *Understanding Soviet Military Developments* (April 1977; processed), p. 20.

a. There are also twenty mobilization divisions (including at least one airborne unit) that are under strength but assigned full division equipment sets.

sions, and a doubling of the artillery assets in both motorized rifle units and armored divisions. The net effect has been to further increase the shock power of the GSFG, which remains the preeminent combat force in Europe.

Qualitative improvements in equipment for Soviet ground forces have also been impressive. New tanks and armored personnel carriers, clearly superior in design to their predecessors, have been deployed. Soviet armored personnel carriers now mount cannons and antitank weapons, the first in any army to do so. The mobility of Soviet forces is improved because towed artillery has been augmented with self-propelled units and because mobile gun and missile air defense systems have been introduced. These new weapons finally provide the mobility and firepower needed to generate the shock power and achieve the rapid advance long emphasized in Soviet military doctrine.

Naval Forces

Since 1964 the Soviet Navy has accounted for a relatively steady and relatively small (less than 20 percent) share of the Soviet defense budget. As a result, from 1964 to 1976 the number of major surface combatants dropped by about 5 percent, the number of minor surface combatants by nearly 35 percent, and the number of submarines by 35 percent. Still, despite its smaller size, the Soviet Navy is a more capable force today than it was in 1964. Aggregate tonnage, a crude measure of capabilities, increased considerably, and there were sharp jumps in the number of surface-to-surface and surface-to-air missile systems deployed on Soviet warships. Conventional submarines were

Table 6. Soviet Naval General Purpose Forces and Capabilities, 1964 and 1976

Description	1964	1976
Aircraft carriers	0	1
Helicopter cruisers	0	2
Cruisers	20	31
Destroyers	114	87
Frigates	102	107
Minor combatants carrying missiles	110	137
Minor combatants	700	391
Conventional submarines	371	176
Nuclear submarines	22	78
Amphibious ships	12	82
Minesweepers	450	365
Other[a]	250	255
Total displacement (millions of tons)	2.2	2.6
Surface-to-surface missile launchers	456	1,294
Surface-to-air missile rails	20	302
Area (long-range) antisubmarine weapons	0	160

Sources: Authors' estimates derived from IISS, *The Military Balance, 1964–1965*, pp. 5–6; *Jane's Fighting Ships, 1965–1966* (McGraw-Hill, 1965), pp. 425–46; IISS, *The Military Balance, 1976–1977*, pp. 8–9; *Jane's Fighting Ships, 1976–1977* (McGraw-Hill, 1976), pp. 688–753; and *Fiscal Year 1978 Authorization for Military Procurement*, Hearings, pt. 2, p. 945.

a. Includes a variety of support ships, such as intelligence collection vessels, oilers, repair ships, and depot ships.

replaced with nuclear-powered submarines. Moreover, a new type of weapon system—area (long-range) antisubmarine torpedo and rocket launchers—first appeared on Soviet warships during the period and have been deployed extensively since. These changes are summarized in table 6.

The primary mission of the Soviet Navy continues to be defensive: to protect the Soviet Union from Western sea-based strike forces and to deter the latter from intervening in regions, like the Middle East, close to Soviet shores. In the first instance, Soviet naval forces are directed against Western aircraft carrier task groups deployed in waters such as the Mediterranean, where their aircraft are capable of striking Soviet territory. As the range of these carrier-based aircraft has grown, Soviet naval forces have had to be deployed further and further from Soviet territory to carry out this mission.

Increasingly in recent years, however, the threat to the USSR from the seas has originated not from the aircraft carrier but from the strategic submarine. The Soviet Union also has deployed a considerable portion of its strategic capabilities at sea in submarines. Accordingly, emphasis in Soviet naval construction and operations has turned more and more to antisubmarine warfare—both to protect

Soviet strategic submarines and to be able to destroy Western strategic submarines should a nuclear exchange appear imminent.

By virtually all accounts, the Soviet Navy poses little threat to Western submarines. However, the recent deployment of the first *Kuril*-class aircraft carrier (three more *Kurils* are under construction) could help Soviet strategic submarines penetrate the barriers that Western navies would establish in attempts to prevent the submarines from reaching their operating areas in times of crisis or war.

Of course, the Soviet Navy could be used for many other missions. In the event of war in Europe, its attack submarines could attempt to isolate the continent, preventing U.S. reinforcements and supplies from arriving in time. In peacetime, the Soviet Navy promotes Soviet interests abroad, supports Soviet foreign policy, and counters Western efforts at "gunboat diplomacy." On the other hand, there are some things that the Soviet Navy cannot do because it continues to lack capabilities essential to projecting Soviet power into distant regions against opposition: significant sea-based air power, amphibious assault capabilities, underway replenishment and at-sea repair capabilities, an extensive network of overseas bases, and greater endurance in its warships.

Air Forces

The Soviet Union maintains five separate air components, each with a special mission. As shown in table 7, the relative emphasis given to each changed markedly between 1964 and 1976.

As noted, the air defense forces have been de-emphasized, suffering a one-third cut in strength. The main beneficiary of this reallocation of resources was Frontal Aviation—the tactical air arm, whose missions are to support Soviet ground forces by attacking maneuvering NATO forces and to stage independent air strikes against immobile targets such as airfields. Frontal Aviation's fixed-wing assets were increased by about one-third; its load-carrying capacity was more than doubled. Like the ground forces they support, about one-half of Frontal Aviation's aircraft are deployed for European operations and one-fourth for the Far East; the remainder are held in reserve.

These changes in the size and capability of Frontal Aviation reflect significant changes in Soviet military doctrine. In the past, Soviet tactical aviation was controlled directly by the ground forces or used for defensive operations behind the battle lines. Now, Soviet ground

Table 7. Soviet Air Forces and Their Composition, 1964 and 1976

	1964		1976	
Description	*Fixed wing*	*Helicopters*	*Fixed wing*	*Helicopters*
Air Defense Command				
Number of aircraft	4,040	...	2,590	...
Total weight (millions of pounds)[a]	65.6	...	86.4	...
Naval Aviation				
Number of aircraft	800	200	950	250
Long-Range Aviation				
Number of aircraft	1,100	...	849	...
Frontal Aviation				
Number of aircraft	3,360	n.a.	4,600	2,950
Offensive load-carrying capacity (millions of ton-miles)[b]	1.2	...	3.2	...
Military Transport Aviation				
Number of aircraft	1,700	790	1,550	320
Total lift (millions of ton-miles)[c]	9.5	n.a.	25.8	n.a.

Sources: Authors' estimates derived from James D. Hessman, "The Soviet Union Moves Ahead: On Land, On the Sea, and In the Air," *Armed Forces Journal* (August 17, 1970), p. 34; IISS, *The Military Balance, 1976–77*, p. 10; *Allocation of Resources in the Soviet Union and China—1975*, Hearings before the Subcommittee on Priorities and Economy in Government of the Joint Economic Committee, 94:1 (GPO, 1975), pt. 1, p. 148; and William Green and Gordon Swanborough, *The Observer's Soviet Aircraft Directory* (Frederic Warne, 1975).

n.a. Not available.

a. A rough measure of aggregate capability; heavier aircraft often have greater range and carry more avionics and air-to-air missiles. The relation between weight and capability is influenced by numerous factors, however, including the materials used to construct the aircraft, engine efficiency, and the aircraft's design.

b. The product of combat radius and payload, summed over all Frontal Aviation aircraft.

c. The product of combat range and lift capacity per day, summed over all airlift aircraft assigned to Military Transport Aviation.

forces themselves are responsible for gaining air superiority over the battlefield and providing fire support to front-line troops through the use of mobile gun and missile air defense systems, artillery, and rockets. Freed of its past defensive responsibilities, Frontal Aviation is being equipped with aircraft with lesser dog-fighting capabilities but longer ranges and larger payloads. By the early 1980s, it will be able to launch conventional strikes at primary NATO airbases, nuclear storage sites, and command-and-control facilities at the onset of a European war. Such an attack could severely cripple NATO.[3]

Increases in the strength of Soviet military units and improvements in Soviet weapon systems are not sufficient reason to spend more

3. Changes in Soviet air forces are described in detail in Robert P. Berman, *Soviet Air Power in Transition* (Brookings Institution, 1977).

money on U.S. military forces. For one thing, gains in Soviet military capabilities must be judged in light of past and prospective changes in U.S. and allied military capabilities; they are constantly improving, too. Needed are net assessments of relative capabilities—judgments about the changes likely to occur in the military balance should present trends continue—and of the consequences of the changes that seem likely. Obviously, when Soviet military capabilities do not directly threaten U.S. interests—for instance, forces on the Chinese border—a Soviet gain may not require a U.S. response. Judgments like these are discussed in the two sections that follow; first for strategic nuclear forces and then for general purpose (conventional) forces.

The Strategic Balance

Since 1960 U.S. strategic offensive forces have had three components. Land-based ICBMs now consist of 1,000 Minuteman missiles and 54 older Titan missiles. Five hundred and fifty of the Minuteman missiles are equipped with MIRVs, usually three reentry vehicles per missile. These systems permit each missile to deliver nuclear warheads to a number of targets spaced quite far apart. Sea-based strategic forces consist of thirty-one Poseidon and ten Polaris nuclear-powered submarines, each carrying sixteen intermediate-range SLBMs. The missiles on the Poseidon submarines also carry MIRVs. Strategic bomber forces consist of twenty squadrons of B-52 long-range heavy bombers armed with air-to-surface missiles and gravity bombs, plus four squadrons of intermediate-range FB-111 bombers similarly armed.

Together, the three offensive components form what is known as the triad. Because each system depends on different techniques to assure its survivability against a Soviet first strike or its ability to penetrate Soviet defenses, each is believed to be capable of carrying out a retaliatory mission independently. The maintenance of these relatively independent capabilities in three separate components is a hedge against the sudden appearance of countermeasures that would negate the effectiveness of any two of the components.

Each of these strategic components is now being modernized at substantial cost. Between fiscal 1975 and 1978 spending for the procurement of strategic weapon systems increased by $2.8 billion in constant 1978 dollars. By the early 1980s annual real expenditures for strategic forces could rise by another $3 billion to $5 billion.

Specifics of the modernization program are outlined below.

ICBMs. A higher-yield warhead known as the Mark 12A has been designed for Minuteman missiles, and the missile's guidance system is being improved to increase its accuracy. These measures will greatly improve the capability of the Minuteman force to destroy hardened targets. Minuteman silos also have been upgraded to improve their hardness and survivability.

At the same time, a new ICBM—the M-X—is being developed to replace Minuteman. Under present plans, the M-X would be mobile, designed to move along hardened and covered trenches. Because the precise location of any one M-X would not be known, many warheads would have to be fired at each trench to be sure of destroying the missile inside. Thus, deployment of this weapon system could offset any gain in the USSR's ability to destroy hardened targets. The M-X would also provide the United States with much greater capability for destroying hardened targets because it could carry more and larger warheads than Minuteman. Under the Ford 1978 budget, the M-X missile would attain an initial operational capability in December of 1983, one year earlier than was envisioned in the fiscal 1977 program. The Carter budget restored the program to its former schedule.

The decision whether to acquire the M-X missile, and if so, what specific characteristics it should have, will be the single most important weapon system decision faced by the Carter administration. The program will be extremely expensive, primarily because of the cost of constructing the trenches. Preliminary estimates indicate that it would cost around $34 billion to deploy a force of 300 missiles; 40 percent of this amount would be used for construction. More important, the design of the missile is at the heart of the dispute over U.S. strategic planning and force posture. Because mobile missiles greatly complicate the verification of arms control agreements, the United States has resisted building such weapons for many years, making a unilateral statement in connection with the 1972 strategic arms limitation talks (SALT) agreements that it would consider the deployment of land-mobile missiles as violating the spirit of these accords. This philosophy obviously has changed in recent years, mainly because of concern about the survivability of fixed-site ICBMs like Minuteman.

SLBMs. The present U.S. force of strategic submarines was constructed between 1959 and 1967. Because submarines generally require about five years to build and last about twenty to twenty-five years, new submarines must be authorized now if the SLBM force is to remain at its present size. Such a program has been pursued for several years. Eleven new *Ohio*-class submarines have been authorized already; two more were requested for fiscal 1978 in both the Ford and the Carter budgets. The *Ohio* class is much larger than existing Poseidon submarines and carries 50 percent more missiles. It will also be faster, quieter, and capable of operating at greater depths than present strategic submarines.

A new missile is also being built—the Trident I. This missile would be deployed on *Ohio*-class submarines and also retrofitted into ten existing Poseidon submarines. Trident I missiles, which would carry MIRVs, would have a range of about 4,000 nautical miles; the Poseidon's range is 3,000 miles or so. A second generation Trident missile—Trident II—is in a much earlier research stage. This missile would have a 6,000-mile range and potentially could be much more accurate than Trident I if fitted, as has been suggested, with maneuvering reentry vehicles.[4]

Bombers. The Air Force planned to replace existing strategic bombers with the B-1, a high performance aircraft designed to penetrate the dense and technologically sophisticated Soviet air defenses that are expected to exist toward the end of the century. The Ford program envisioned buying 244 B-1 bombers; the first eight production models were included in the fiscal 1978 budget. The Carter budget at first reduced the fiscal 1978 request to five aircraft; in June 1977 the President canceled the full program.

Under the Carter program, in the future the manned bomber force would be made up of older FB-111s and B-52s that would penetrate Soviet air defenses, as well as B-52s and a new type of aircraft armed with cruise missiles that would stand off from enemy defenses. The cruise missiles would saturate enemy defenses while short-range

---

4. Maneuvering reentry vehicles would be powered and guided during the final stages of their flight, rather than falling freely on a ballistic trajectory as do existing reentry vehicles.

attack missiles on the penetrating bombers would be used to attack targets that are heavily defended by surface-to-air missiles.

Cruise missiles. These new weapons have more far-reaching implications. Two cruise missiles are now under development. The Air Force program would produce an air-launched missile to be carried in bombers. The missile emerging from the Navy program, Tomahawk, could be deployed on aircraft, on surface ships, on submarines (from which it could be fired through the torpedo tubes), or on mobile ground launchers. If this missile were deployed on a ship or ground launcher, it in effect would add a fourth offensive component to the U.S. strategic force posture. Upon canceling the B-1, the President decided to accelerate cruise missile development.

U.S. strategic air defenses. These also are being modernized. Both force levels and a planned modernization program for air defenses were cut back sharply following the 1972 SALT agreements. All surface-to-air missiles previously assigned to the Continental Air Defense Command have been phased out of the force structure; the number of interceptor aircraft has also been reduced. At present, U.S. strategic defensive forces include only six interceptor aircraft squadrons on active duty and eleven squadrons assigned to the Air National Guard, and several early warning systems. There are other aircraft and some surface-to-air missiles located in the United States that would provide air defense in the event of an attack, but for one reason or another these forces are not counted in the strategic category.

The continuing momentum in the Soviet strategic program and particularly the development of the Backfire bomber have led to new pressure to rebuild U.S. continental air defenses. The first explicit result of this pressure was included in President Ford's 1978 budget: $30 million to initiate the procurement of F-15 aircraft configured as interceptors to replace the F-106 aircraft now in the force. President Carter's budget proposal deferred this request pending reevaluation of air defense requirements. But two other elements of what had been planned for strategic air defense modernization have continued in development, despite the cutback in strategic air defense, because both also have roles in the general purpose forces; their strategic mission is again coming to the fore. The first is the Airborne Warning and Control System (AWACS), which is viewed as a survivable way both to detect low-flying aircraft and to ensure command and control

Table 8. Indexes of U.S. Strategic Capabilities in 1977, and upon Completion of the M-X, Trident, and Bomber Programs

Description	1977	Modernized[a]
Force levels (launchers)	2,127	1,945
Missiles only	1,710	1,720
Throw-weight (millions of pounds)[b]	9.26	10.89
Missiles only	5.06	6.90
Independently targetable warheads		
(missile reentry vehicles and bombs)	8,557	14,850
Missiles only	6,823	9,960
Equivalent megatonnage[c]	2,847	5,941
Missiles only	1,905	3,737

Sources: Authors' estimates derived from IISS, *The Military Balance, 1976–1977*, pp. 5, 106–08; "Annual Defense Department Report for FY 1978," pp. 58–79; *Full Committee Consideration of Overall National Security Programs and Related Budget Requirements*, Hearings before the House Committee on the Armed Services, 94:1 (GPO, 1975), pp. 228, 247; Donald E. Fink, "Minuteman Experience Aiding MX," *Aviation Week and Space Technology*, vol. 105 (July 19, 1976), pp. 113–20; and Clarence A. Robinson, Jr., "New Propellant Evaluated for Trident Second Stage," *Aviation Week and Space Technology*, vol. 103 (October 13, 1975), pp. 15–19.

a. The "modernized force" is assumed to be consistent with the constraints imposed by the 1974 Vladivostok accord. It consists of 300 M-X ICBMs, 300 Minuteman III ICBMs, and 720 Trident SLBMs, for a total of 1,320 MIRV-carrying missiles; plus 400 Minuteman II ICBMs and 225 bombers. Although some B-52s and FB-111s are retained in the force, a cruise-missile-carrying aircraft is projected for this time frame. If Trident II were introduced, there would be a 22 percent increase in missile throw-weight and a 21 percent increase in total throw-weight; a 43 percent increase in missile warheads and a 29 percent increase in total warheads; and a 43 percent increase in missile equivalent megatonnage and a 27 percent increase in total equivalent megatonnage.

b. The weight-carrying capacity of missiles and bombers is not directly comparable. This index includes the payload of each system that could be used to carry nuclear weapons, its protective structure, and associated guidance system.

c. Equivalent megatonnage is a measure of the area destruction capacity of a nuclear arsenal based on the number and explosive yields of its various component weapons and the fact that the extent of the ground area that would be destroyed by a nuclear explosion does not increase one-to-one with increases in the yield of the nuclear warhead.

of the air defense battle. The purchase of nineteen of these aircraft has already been authorized, ostensibly to be used in Europe. But Air Force spokesmen state that of the twenty-eight AWACS aircraft the United States plans to buy, only seven would be earmarked for NATO. Four more would be used for air defense over the North Atlantic, and the remainder would be designated for the defense of North America—strategic air defense. NATO requirements are to be filled by additional AWACS aircraft purchased by European nations. Second, a new and very capable surface-to-air missile system, known as Patriot, also is continuing in development. This system is being developed primarily for use on NATO battlefields, but it could also be used for continental air defense should a decision be taken to rebuild the U.S. system.

Together, these programs would substantially increase U.S. strategic capabilities. Although the total number of strategic launchers (missiles and bombers) would decline somewhat, completion of the M-X and new bomber programs and replacement of the Polaris/ Poseidon force with Tridents would significantly increase the throw-weight, number of warheads, and equivalent megatonnage of U.S. strategic forces. This is shown in table 8.

The cost would run high. Modernizing the bomber force could cost $10 billion; the M-X program would require at least $34 billion; and to build up to a force of thirty Trident submarines would mean expenditures of roughly another $25 billion. Modernizing the air defense system would add more. Obviously, many other uses could be found for this money, in both the defense and the domestic sectors. Thus, it is well to ask what eventualities these programs are designed to meet and whether they are likely to accomplish their purposes.

In recent years, Soviet strategic deployments have given rise to two kinds of concern in the United States.

The most specific pertains to an expected Soviet advantage in the two nations' relative ability to destroy hardened targets. Aside from the greater number of missiles in its inventory, the Soviet Union has the advantage in that its missiles are larger than those of the United States (have greater "throw-weight"). This means that Soviet missiles, when equipped with MIRVs, could carry more warheads than U.S. missiles or that each Soviet warhead could have a greater yield, or both. The generation of Soviet missiles now being deployed has accentuated this superior throw-weight. Assuming that eventually the Soviet Union masters the various techniques necessary to achieve the high accuracies that characterize U.S. missiles, sometime in the next decade, unless changes are made in the U.S. force posture, the USSR would have a decided advantage in relative capability for destroying hardened targets, notably missile silos. In extreme crises, it is argued, this superiority would give the USSR more options than would be available to the United States. It could, for example, use a portion of its ICBM force in a first strike against U.S. ICBMs, deterring a U.S. response against Soviet cities or military facilities by dint of the large number of missiles that would remain available to answer any U.S. retaliation. Moreover, the argument goes, such exchanges need not actually occur to have an effect on the course of world affairs. Such Soviet superiority in "hard-target kill capabilities" supposedly could make the United States timid and the Soviet Union bold when confrontations occurred, leading to outcomes unfavorable to the United States.

Although improvements to the Minuteman force will help, the M-X program is the primary way in which the Department of Defense plans to offset this projected Soviet advantage. According to the department, deployment of the M-X would enable the United States to nearly match Soviet "hard-target kill capabilities" throughout the 1980s. Even without the M-X, U.S. hard-target kill capabilities are expected to remain greater than those of the Soviet Union until 1983, the result primarily of deployment of the Minuteman Mark 12A reentry vehicle and improvements in the Minuteman guidance system. Beyond 1983, however, the USSR is expected to outpace the United States in this aspect of the strategic competition unless M-X is deployed. That Soviet capabilities are not expected to rise sharply until 1983 indicates that the ICBMs now being deployed by the USSR are not sufficiently accurate to destroy hardened targets effectively.

Recent changes in the strategic balance have also evoked a less specific, less tangible sort of concern in some Americans—that the sheer pace and range of Soviet strategic developments will soon result in a worldwide image of Soviet power in the ascendant. Although specialists are aware that U.S. strategic capabilities have improved significantly since 1964, these changes have been far less dramatic than the regular unveiling of new Soviet missiles, and it may appear that the United States is being overwhelmed. Such impressions, superficial though they may be, presumably could have political consequences if they became widespread.

At the extreme, such concern is transformed into a fear that the USSR is seeking a capability to fight and survive a nuclear war. Hard-target kill capabilities are an important element in these calculations. Other elements include the enormous resources that the Soviet Union devotes to strategic air defenses, the Soviet civil defense program, and various other programs such as experiments with techniques for destroying early warning satellites. Typically, the war is envisioned as opening with a preemptive Soviet missile attack on U.S. ICBMs, strategic submarine bases, bomber bases, and command-and-control facilities. At the end of this initial salvo, the supposition goes, all that would be left of U.S. strategic forces would be the 30 percent of the bomber force that is maintained on alert, and the twenty or so strategic submarines that are usually at sea. The former, it is argued, would suffer such heavy losses from Soviet air defenses that they would be unable to carry out more than a small part of their retaliatory mission. The latter—though likely to survive any attempt to find and destroy them—carry missiles with warheads that are too small to do much damage against a Soviet society protected by extensive civil defenses. Again, as in worries about Soviet superiority in hard-target kill capabilities, the concern is not so much that such a war will actually come about but rather that if such a situation became plausible U.S. political influence would be severely weakened.

Implications of the U.S. strategic modernization program for these broad political concerns are difficult to assess. Introduction of cruise missiles would improve the bomber force's ability to saturate advanced Soviet air defenses, should they be developed. The greater throw-weight of Trident II would permit the deployment of higher-yield warheads on U.S. SLBMs, so that submarines surviving a Soviet first strike could inflict greater damage on Soviet society, regardless of civil defense preparations. U.S. air defense modernization would provide some shield against the marginal threat posed by the Backfire. In short, each of the measures would reduce whatever limited ability the Soviet Union developed to wage a nuclear war and survive. Taken together, the U.S. programs should help to erase the image of Soviet strategic momentum, with all that might portend for international behavior during crises and at more peaceful times. Still, questions remain: whether the worries just described are realistic or more in the nature of phantoms created by U.S. decisionmakers to which they are now reacting; and if these worries are well founded, are there less costly ways to respond?

Are the Worries Realistic?

There seems little doubt that one fear—a growing image of Soviet momentum and ascendancy in the strategic field—is well founded. Increasingly, statements by public officials in this country and abroad and opinion polls of the general population indicate awareness of and concern about the scope and pace of the Soviet strategic buildup. It is not clear to what extent the Soviet Union itself shares the view that it is gaining the upper hand in the strategic balance, but it cannot have failed to note the apprehension in the West, and that in itself might lead it to behave rashly under certain circumstances. Although the links between perceptions of relative strategic capabilities and foreign policy behavior are not well understood, the fact that many decision-makers around the world believe such links exist is sufficient reason for prudent defense planners not to discount the phenomenon.

Concern about Soviet hard-target kill capabilities is less easily substantiated. The size and number of its ICBMs certainly provide the Soviet Union with a theoretical ability to destroy most of the United States' ICBMs in a first strike, once it masters the techniques necessary to improve the accuracy of its missiles. But carrying out a preemptive first strike is likely to prove far more difficult in practice than in theory. Such a military operation would require split-second timing and coordination, and its effectiveness would be influenced by factors of which we know very little—such as the effects of the first nuclear explosions on warheads arriving later, the reliability of missiles, and so forth.

Moreover, an examination of official statements on relative hard-target kill capabilities over the past few years indicates a proclivity on the part of the United States to emphasize potential Soviet capabilities and to underestimate its own. For example, U.S. officials do not now expect Soviet hard-target kill capabilities to increase significantly until 1982 whereas improvements to Minuteman will soon augment U.S. capabilities; however, statements of U.S. defense officials over the past five to ten years left a more alarming impression.

The most extreme fear—the potential Soviet capacity to fight and survive a nuclear war—is clearly farfetched. The assumptions underlying it present a most optimistic picture from the Soviet perspective and a most pessimistic one for the United States. It is assumed, among other things, that the difficulties of mounting a coordinated, massive attack on U.S. nuclear forces are overcome, that the large number of Soviet weapons that would be involved work reasonably well, that the United States does not launch its own ICBMs upon warning of an attack, that the Soviet Union overcomes the so far impossible task of reliably detecting and intercepting bombers penetrating at low altitudes, and—most incredibly—that civil defenses, such as evacuating cities, are sufficient to protect most of the Soviet population from the nearly 3,000 warheads expected to be launched from U.S. submarines operating at sea and thus surviving the attack, and that these civil defense measures do not, while in preparation, alert the United States that something is afoot.

Moreover, even though those who cling to this worry state that they fear not so much the eventuality of such a war as what forecasts of such capabilities might mean for U.S. political influence, the premise remains the same—that Soviet leaders would gauge the risks associated with this remote combination of assumptions as low enough to make them willing to push hard during serious political confrontations, believing that, should matters by some extreme chance go against them, the Soviet Union could fight a nuclear war and survive relatively well. It is difficult to conceive of a Soviet leader reaching such a conclusion—to rest the fate of his nation and to risk 50 million or 100 million fatalities—on the basis of computer simulations and elaborate assumptions about the course of nuclear war. Certainly no sane person would make such a decision.

How Should the United States Respond?

In view of this assessment, how should the United States respond to the Soviet strategic buildup? Although it is not possible to evaluate each aspect of the U.S. strategic program in this chapter, a few general guidelines may be suggested.

1. Proposed strategic programs would do little to specifically counter the additional threats to the United States posed by new Soviet strategic capabilities. At worst, there is even a slight risk that some aspects of the U.S. program might actually increase the risk of nuclear war by making the Soviet Union fear for the survivability of its own ICBMs, thus giving it additional incentive to strike first in a crisis. At best, programs to modernize U.S. strategic forces can only offset the feared political effects of Soviet strategic advantages. There is only one way to actually reduce the nuclear threat to this nation, and that is to negotiate agreements in which the United States and the Soviet Union mutually reduce strategic force levels and eliminate weapons like fixed-site ICBMs that, because of their potential vulnerability, invite instability in the strategic balance. Thus first priority should be given to the SALT negotiations, which should attempt to achieve significant reductions in strategic force levels and restraints in weapon modernization programs.

2. In evaluating proposed weapon programs, careful considera-

tion must therefore be given to their possible effects on the negotiations. This cuts two ways. Some programs may complicate the negotiations or make it difficult for the USSR to accept a freeze on current capabilities; this may have been the case with the U.S. deployment of MIRVs before the 1972 agreement, for example. At the same time, it seems clear that there must be sufficient momentum in the U.S. strategic program to make the Soviet Union perceive advantages in limiting its own forces.

3. If there is one dimension of the strategic arms competition in which the United States has always maintained an advantage, it is in technology. Soviet missiles may be larger and more numerous, but U.S. missiles are more accurate, more combat-ready, and more efficient.[5] Moreover, the United States has generally been the first to introduce new types of systems—from the atomic bomb itself to MIRVs. Thus, to some extent, the United States may retain a decided advantage over the USSR, which probably has some political impact, in that it is widely believed to be the leader in weapons technology.

Today, that advantage seems to have crystallized in the cruise missile. Just as the USSR is deploying a new generation of SLBMs and ICBMs that are roughly comparable to their U.S. counterparts, this nation has come up with a new type of system which, as the USSR is well aware, promises to enable it to deploy—at relatively low cost—a large number of additional strategic weapons. Thus, the cruise missile programs could provide a potent lever for the United States in the negotiations, one that could be used to wrest serious Soviet concessions in areas that concern the United States, such as missile throw-weight.

4. Because of the time remaining before the USSR deploys forces with significant hard-target kill capabilities, even according to what are probably conservative Defense Department estimates, it is not necessary to move immediately to augment U.S. capabilities in this area. The new Minuteman reentry vehicle and guidance improvements are probably sensible, but development of the M-X need not be accelerated as was envisioned in the Ford 1978 budget. Rather, the United States can afford to develop the M-X at a more leisurely (and more efficient) pace, looking to the SALT negotiations to eliminate the problem before it becomes a reality. Similarly, there seems

---

5. Efficiency is not just a matter of pride. More efficient rocket engines, guidance and control software, and warhead designs may mean that smaller missiles could carry greater destructive power.

to be no need at present to develop the Trident II missile and its proposed maneuvering reentry vehicle beyond preliminary conceptual studies.

5. Finally, the need to augment U.S. strategic offensive and defensive capabilities on the basis of broad and undifferentiated worries about Soviet war-fighting capabilities is not a compelling one. There are risks in the future strategic balance, but none so serious as to warrant a crash program to build up U.S. capabilities. Proposals to modernize the U.S. forces—like the M-X and Trident—can be examined carefully and compared with alternative ways of replacing the forces that, because of age or technological obsolescence, will have to be taken out of service.

The Balance of Conventional Forces

Unlike strategic forces, U.S. and Soviet conventional (or general purpose) forces do not threaten each other's territory directly. Instead, these forces are arrayed against each other in third areas, where trends in the balance of U.S. and Soviet conventional military capabilities are believed to have a significant impact on the course of world events. Three such areas are most important: Europe, the Middle East, and East Asia.

The Military Balance in Europe*

The importance of Europe to the security and economic and political well-being of the United States has been discussed at length in various editions of the annual Brookings publication, *Setting National Priorities*. U.S. armed forces play three roles in protecting these interests.

By balancing Soviet power and deterring Soviet adventures, U.S. forces in Europe have permitted political rapprochement between East and West to develop and continue.

By making credible U.S. guarantees for the security of Western Europe, U.S. forces have helped avoid West German perception of a need to develop nuclear weapons, thus also facilitating East-West rapprochement and greater cooperation among the nations of Western Europe.

Finally, the presence of sizable U.S. forces in Europe has strength-

---

* This section was prepared by Frederick W. Young.

Table 9. The Balance of Forces in Northern and Central Europe, 1970 and 1976

	NATO			Warsaw Pact		
Component	1970	1976	Change (percent)	1970	1976	Change (percent)
Combat and direct support troops (thousands)	580	635	9	900	910	1
Tanks (number deployed with units)	5,500	7,000	27	14,000	19,000	35
Tactical aircraft	2,200	2,100	−5	3,940	4,200	6
Tactical nuclear warheads[a]	7,000	7,000	0	3,500	3,500	0

Source: IISS, *The Military Balance, 1970–1971* and *1976–1977*.
a. Warsaw Pact figures have not been verified in official sources.

ened the close economic and political cooperation that now characterizes relations between the United States and Western Europe.

TRENDS IN THE EUROPEAN BALANCE. Most public comment on the military situation in Europe emphasizes a decade-long buildup in Warsaw Pact forces. Yet focusing solely on Pact capabilities ignores the substantial efforts of NATO nations to improve their own military capabilities. NATO's military position vis-à-vis the Warsaw Pact clearly weakened during the late 1960s when the Soviet Union substantially increased its conventional forces in Eastern Europe. But since about 1970 both sides have been expanding and modernizing their forces at comparable rates. As a result, gross comparisons of force levels, like the one in table 9, show no significant change in the balance of forces so far in the 1970s.

Changes in the balance of forces resulting from the modernization of weapon systems are more difficult to assess, yet in side-by-side comparisons of similar weapons' technology, NATO appears to have done rather well.

First, the modernization of Warsaw Pact air forces has been substantially matched by NATO. While the Warsaw Pact has acquired more new combat aircraft in the last few years, the aircraft acquired by NATO can carry a larger total payload. Other improvements, such as those in avionics and precision-guided ordnance, also have favored NATO.

Second, both sides have been modernizing their armored forces. The Soviet Union has produced about 17,000 tanks since 1970, including 2,000 of the new T-72 design. NATO has acquired about 4,000 new tanks during this period—mostly the U.S. M-60 and the

West German Leopard I, both of which appear to be as capable as the T-72. The Warsaw Pact, which traditionally has emphasized armor, continues to have about three times the tank inventory of NATO, but NATO has made impressive strides in closing the gap in tank production rates—the ratio by which NATO is outproduced having been cut from about 4:1 to about 2:1.

Third, increases in antitank capabilities seem roughly balanced. NATO's antitank guided missiles are considerably easier to operate and have shorter flight times than those deployed by the Warsaw Pact. Shorter flight times are a significant advantage because they increase the probability that the antitank gunner will be able to guide the missile to its target before the target disappears from his view and because they reduce the amount of time the gunner must remain exposed to enemy observation and fire. On the other hand, Pact antitank gunners enjoy greater protection from artillery and small arms fire because their weapons are more often designed to be operated from inside armored vehicles.

Fourth, improvements in air defense capabilities also appear roughly balanced. Since 1970 the Soviet Union has introduced four mobile air defense missile systems, which, along with continued procurement of previously introduced items such as the ZSU-23-4 air defense gun, have greatly increased the protection offered by Pact air defenses to combat units on the front lines. This specific effort has not been matched by NATO. However, with NATO's deployment of very capable fighter aircraft such as the F-15, its air combat capabilities have increased more than those of the Warsaw Pact.

Fifth, both sides have deployed roughly comparable tank-destroying helicopters.

Sixth, the Soviet Union has doubled the number of artillery tubes with its forces; NATO has increased its artillery capabilities by developing substantially more effective artillery munitions.

The list could go on, but it seems evident—within the limits of uncertainties surrounding any such assessments—that the modernization of Warsaw Pact forces has been effectively matched by NATO improvements. Even if one accepts this conclusion, however, a question remains: have the characteristics of these new weapons changed the nature of warfare in a way that would favor one side or the other? Two hypotheses seem to have gained wide acceptance: (1) new weapons have increased the rates at which matériel would be destroyed and consumed in battle; and (2) the expected ratio of combat losses has shifted in favor of defensive ground forces at the expense of attacking ground and air forces.[6]

In Europe, the second hypothesis favors NATO, which, despite the necessity for counterattacks, is likely to be on the defensive more than the Warsaw Pact. The first hypothesis, however, favors Warsaw Pact efforts to achieve a quick victory before NATO reinforcements could be mobilized. Combined with long-standing concern about a mismatch between the Soviet emphasis on short wars and NATO preparations for more protracted conflicts, this presumption that battle in Europe would result in heavy losses and the rapid consumption of matériel has contributed to current misgivings about the adequacy of NATO's defenses should it fall victim to a surprise attack.

In effect, the current balance of forces is such that neither side could be guaranteed a favorable outcome should war break out in Europe. Assuming that the Warsaw Pact would begin to mobilize for war before NATO did, its greatest military advantage would exist in the first few days of a crisis. Thereafter, if an uninterrupted buildup of forces were to continue on both sides, the ratio of opposing combat forces available in Europe would continue to shift in NATO's favor unless the Soviet Union were willing to move large numbers of troops from its Central, Southern, and Far Eastern military districts—an unlikely development in view of the threat from China. In the very long term, the ratio would probably continue to shift in NATO's favor because of its far larger population and economic base and consequently greater potential for raising and supporting military forces.

Because of these disadvantages, the most attractive strategy for the Warsaw Pact would be an attempt to achieve victory in the shortest possible time—not surprisingly, the very strategy advocated by Soviet military doctrine. The chances of success in such an effort would ob-

6. For the most part, these hypotheses are based on the demonstrated effectiveness of antitank guided missiles, surface-to-air missiles, and air defense guns in the 1973 Arab-Israeli war. Three factors, though, should make one wary of drawing too sharp a comparison between October 1973 and a future war in Europe. First, changes in tactics made during the 1973 war reduced then, and others proposed since would reduce still further, the effectiveness of these new weapons. Second, weather and terrain in the Middle East provide far better visibility for the location and identification of targets than would be the case in Europe. Finally, weapons employed in the 1973 war were generally less capable than similar but more modern weapons now being deployed in Europe by both the Warsaw Pact and NATO.

viously be greatly enhanced if the Warsaw Pact were able to achieve strategic and tactical surprise.

THE RISK OF SURPRISE ATTACK. The Warsaw Pact could initiate a surprise attack on Western Europe with either nuclear or conventional weapons. If the USSR were willing to use nuclear weapons, its forces clearly would have the capability of destroying most of NATO's military resources in nearly simultaneous attacks. Warsaw Pact ground forces would then be able to occupy what was left of Western Europe without facing major opposition. However, since the uncertainties involved in any nuclear war—particularly the risk that the West's response would be to destroy Soviet cities—are great, a surprise nuclear attack would seem to be an attractive military option for the Soviet Union only if it should believe that war was necessary and that a conventional attack would inevitably escalate to large-scale nuclear warfare.

A more likely possibility would be a surprise attack with conventional forces. If all Pact forces in Eastern Europe were to attack at full strength without warning, existing NATO forces would doubtless be faced with the unfortunate choice of yielding substantial territory or using nuclear weapons. Moreover, the cost of providing conventional capabilities sufficient to stop such an attack would be considerably more than NATO is now willing to spend. But such fears rest on pessimistic assumptions. In reality, the Soviet Union would face severe problems in orchestrating a surprise attack—problems of sufficient magnitude to place an effective conventional defense well within NATO's reach.

It is unrealistic to assume that the ground forces of the Warsaw Pact could launch a major attack without any warning. For one thing, Eastern European army units are manned in peacetime at less than 75 percent full strength. For another, the normal peacetime activities of Soviet ground forces in Eastern Europe, which are believed to be almost fully manned, include training and maintenance activities that at most times would inhibit their immediate availability. Finally, supplies that would be consumed relatively quickly in combat, particularly ammunition and fuel, would have to be distributed to combat units before an attack. In short, Soviet preparations for an attack would probably take at least a few days and Eastern European preparations somewhat longer. These efforts would be noticed by the West almost immediately.

The frequently cited danger that NATO would receive this strategic warning but be unable to react because of political indecision seems exaggerated. There is no doubt that a political decision for NATO to mobilize could take some time—perhaps days. But military commanders of active units have the authority to cancel training and begin preparation for war before that. For example, such steps as loading vehicles, conducting last-minute maintenance, and updating and reviewing operational plans should allow NATO ground forces to begin to move almost immediately after a political decision is reached. Since armored or mechanized forces can travel more than 200 kilometers a day if unopposed, well-prepared forces located as far away as the Benelux countries would have a good chance of reaching defensive positions near the East German border within forty-eight hours of a political decision to mobilize.

The danger of a surprise attack by Warsaw Pact air forces also seems exaggerated. To be sure, aircraft based in Eastern Europe could reach targets in Western Europe after flights of only fifteen to twenty minutes. However, a large-scale air attack could not be conducted without preparations, and would not be conducted before the initiation of preparations for the ground attack. Thus, again without need for a political decision to mobilize, NATO military commanders should have time to shelter aircraft, and possibly to disperse some to auxiliary airfields, as well as to place air defenses on alert.

Another possible indicator of an impending Soviet attack would be the activity of Soviet naval forces. Most of the time, a preponderant fraction of the Soviet Navy is located in the Barents, Baltic, and Black seas, where ships would be of little use for a conflict in Western Europe and where they would be fairly vulnerable to NATO operations to restrict their movements. Accordingly, the Soviet Union would be taking a sizable risk by initiating an attack in Central Europe without first moving much of its Navy into the Mediterranean and the Atlantic. Such a step would require several days to accomplish and would provide NATO with another warning signal.

There would be dangers to NATO even if strategic warning were available. The Soviet Union might decide to build up its forces in Eastern Europe for weeks or even months before initiating an attack. Soviet leaders might decide that stocks pre-positioned near the front lines were too small, that Eastern European forces were too unreliable, or that lines of communication were too vulnerable to guarantee an adequate supply of forces and matériel after the initiation of hostilities. Indeed, despite the military advantages of surprise, the USSR might decide that an overt mobilization effort could provide a show of force sufficient to bring about the favorable settlement of a crisis without war. Even with warning, the longer NATO waited to mobilize, the worse its military situation would become. And the fact that NATO's military position would begin to improve as soon as it took steps to mobilize could in itself provide an incentive for the Warsaw Pact to attack as soon after NATO mobilized as possible. Ironically, this realization might make it difficult for NATO political leaders, hopeful of a peaceful settlement, to decide to mobilize for war.

In summary, the Soviet Union and its allies in the Warsaw Pact could threaten NATO militarily in a number of ways, all of which are unlikely but none of which can be ignored. Present NATO conventional forces would have a good chance of conducting a forward conventional defense if an attack occurred after some period of tension and mobilization on both sides or if the Soviet Union received less than full cooperation from its Eastern European allies. There is room for worry, however, about NATO's capability if all Warsaw Pact forces were committed on short warning or if NATO were slow to mobilize. In these cases, the Warsaw Pact would have a fair, though far from certain, chance of forcing NATO to choose between the first use of nuclear weapons and a large loss of territory. For these reasons, NATO's first priority should be to increase the conventional capabilities of immediately available and readily mobilizable forces.

U.S. PROPOSALS. Five of the proposals in the 1978 budget for strengthening U.S. military forces for Europe are discussed below.

1. *Redeployment of an Army brigade from Southern Germany to the North German Plain.* The best route of advance for a Warsaw Pact armored thrust into Western Germany is through the northern plain. The more mountainous terrain to the south inhibits the mobility of attacking armor and provides better defensive positions for NATO forces. Moreover, NATO forces in southern Germany, which include all U.S. forces, all French forces, and two of four German corps, are stronger and better equipped than those in the north. Thus shifting a U.S. brigade to the north seems a step in the right direc-

tion in that it strengthens the weakest link in NATO's capability to conduct a forward conventional defense on the ground.

2. *Conversion of two active Army infantry divisions and one reserve brigade to mechanized forces.* Present Department of Defense plans to convert infantry forces stationed in the United States to mechanized units are also sound. Although mechanized divisions are more expensive than infantry, their greater capability in the European military environment more than justifies the additional cost. Even the USSR, which by U.S. standards pays a pittance for manpower and a premium for equipment, has chosen to field armored and mechanized forces to the virtual exclusion of infantry.

3. *Increase in stocks of pre-positioned equipment.* A mechanized division can be moved to Europe just as quickly as an infantry division only if its equipment is pre-positioned on the continent. Thus providing equipment stocks in Europe for additional mechanized divisions is an essential element of plans to strengthen NATO's combat capability in the critical initial stages of conflict. This does not require the procurement of additional sets of equipment. For many items, the U.S. Army already plans to buy enough war reserve stocks to provide additional equipment sets for several more divisions.[7] Units based in the United States could train with these war reserve stocks while their own equipment was stored in Europe. Another way to increase pre-positioned stocks without increasing procurement would be to have reserve units share equipment for training.

4. *Increase in strategic airlift capabilities.* The airlift improvement program proposed by the Department of Defense would increase U.S. ability to reinforce forces in Europe in the critical first few weeks following mobilization (table 10). Sealift, though capable of providing many times the capacity of even the improved airlift after three or four weeks of mobilization, simply could not respond during the critical initial period. Pre-positioning equipment in Europe would be another, and in some respects still better, way of accomplishing the same purpose.

The airlift improvement program would increase the amount of matériel that could be shipped from the United States to Europe by air in the first thirty days from about 180,000 tons to about 320,000 tons, for a ten-year cost in excess of $2 billion. The 143,000-ton in-

7. War reserves are stocks of equipment that would be used to replace initial equipment sets lost to enemy action or consumed in battle.

Table 10. Cost of Proposals for Airlift Improvement

Proposal	Ten-year cost (millions of 1976 dollars)	Increase in 30-day capability (thousands of tons)	Cost per ton of increased capability (dollars)
Increased utilization rates of C-5A and C-141 aircraft	1,057	32.5	32,000
Modification of C-141 aircraft	550	19.6	28,000
Modification of commercial aircraft	550	91.0	6,000
Total or average	2,157	143.1	15,000[a]

Source: Comptroller General of the United States, "Information on the Requirement for Strategic Airlift," GAO Report B-162578 (June 8, 1976; processed), p. 7.

a. Average.

crease in capability is roughly equivalent to the weight of the unit equipment of three mechanized infantry divisions. The cost of the program is just about what it would cost to buy the same equipment and store and maintain it in Europe for ten years. Thus, if equipment for mechanized forces is representative cargo and if the amount of matériel available in Europe thirty days after mobilization is the proper measure of merit, buying and storing additional matériel in Europe is about as attractive as the airlift improvement program. Pre-positioning would clearly be the better alternative if it could be accomplished without buying additional equipment, but improved airlift might be necessary to protect U.S. interests in other regions, such as the Middle East. The proposed program should therefore not be judged strictly on the basis of needs for war in Europe.

In any case, certain portions of the airlift program are decidedly worse than others. As shown in table 10, the proposals to increase the utilization rates of C-5A and C-141 military transports and to modify C-141s are about five times as expensive per ton of increased capability as the proposal to modify commercial aircraft. About 60 percent of the proposed increased capability could be obtained for about 25 percent of the total cost if the modification of commercial aircraft were retained and the other proposals were dropped.

5. *Hardening of airbase facilities in Europe.* The most significant element of the proposal to harden airbase facilities in Europe is a plan to construct about 250 aircraft shelters from fiscal 1978 to 1983. The proposed program would increase the number of U.S. shelters in Europe to about 950, enough to accommodate about half the

number of aircraft the United States might reasonably expect to operate in the European theater at any one time. Shelters greatly reduce the vulnerability of aircraft on the ground to air attack and also provide relatively safe places to perform aircraft maintenance. Each shelter normally holds one aircraft, which may have cost as much as $12 million. The estimated cost of each shelter, on the other hand, is about $0.8 million. Thus, until there are sufficient shelters for all expensive combat aircraft, building new shelters would appear to be well worth their cost. This would change if the Soviet Union developed and deployed weapon systems capable of finding and destroying shelters efficiently; that, however, appears unlikely.

The Balance of Forces in the Middle East*

U.S. armed forces serve important purposes in the Mediterranean, the Middle East, and the Indian Ocean. They embody U.S. commitments to the states on the southern flank of NATO. They provide the ultimate guarantee of the survival of Israel. Their acknowledged strength has made it possible for the United States to assume an important role in coaxing both Israelis and Arabs away from violence and toward negotiations. And they stand ready to protect the flow of oil to the United States, its allies, and its friends.

The extent to which the United States honors its commitments in the Middle East and its confidence in its ability to support them militarily have been tested on several occasions, most recently during the October 1973 Arab-Israeli war. There are bound to be future tests of similar importance and danger. In such crises and even in less serious situations, one of the principal elements in the United States' ability to exert its influence effectively has been the perception of local actors and Soviet leaders alike that the United States is both willing and able to prevent the Soviet Union from intervening unilaterally in the region with combat forces.

Neither the United States nor the Soviet Union currently stations combat forces in the Middle East itself, but each maintains a large and powerful naval force in the Mediterranean.[8] These fleets are approximately the same size, although their capabilities differ significantly.

---

* This section was prepared by Robert G. Weinland.

8. Each nation also maintains a smaller naval force in the Indian Ocean. These have little military significance and are not discussed here.

Although its strength can vary widely—especially during international crises—the core of the Soviet Mediterranean Squadron consists of some fifty to fifty-five ships. Roughly half are combatants; of these, about half are submarines and half are various types of surface ships. The remaining twenty-five or so units are auxiliaries. The submarine contingent, which includes both torpedo- and cruise-missile-launching units, provides the Squadron's most effective firepower. Until five years ago the Squadron was supported by reconnaissance, antisubmarine warfare, and missile-launching aircraft operating from bases in Egypt. Since the expulsion of Soviet forces from Egypt in 1972, the Squadron has operated largely without direct air support.

Most of the Squadron's firepower is designed for use primarily against surface ships, principally as a counter to U.S. aircraft carriers—and it poses a serious threat to them. The Squadron also has some capability for antisubmarine warfare, although not enough to significantly threaten U.S. strategic submarines operating in the Mediterranean. If the Soviet Union succeeded in reintroducing land-based naval aircraft in the Mediterranean, their already formidable ability to attack the carriers would receive still another boost, but their antisubmarine capability would not change appreciably.

As matters now stand, the USSR would not find attacking the Sixth Fleet an easy task. Aside from the defensive potential of the carriers' own aircraft, the Sixth Fleet would receive significant additional protection from U.S. Air Force fighter aircraft operating from NATO bases in Italy and Turkey. (More accurately, it could receive such protection if fleet air defense was a priority mission of those aircraft and they had permission of the host nations to carry it out.) At the moment, the nearest Soviet missile-carrying aircraft are based along the northern coast of the Black Sea; to reach and attack targets located in the Mediterranean, they would have to cross NATO-controlled airspace. Even in a non-NATO contingency, once detected attempting to penetrate NATO airspace, they probably would have to fight. Allied air defense capabilities are not insignificant, and Soviet aircraft would probably suffer considerable losses on their way to the Mediterranean.

The size and composition of the Sixth Fleet do not change often. When they do vary, it is not by much. The Sixth Fleet is normally composed of some forty to forty-five units. Three-fourths are combatants, organized into two aircraft carrier task groups and one amphibious landing force; roughly 2,000 Marines are embarked on the latter. A network of underway replenishment and afloat maintenance and repair forces supports all three groups.

In contrast to its Soviet counterpart, the Sixth Fleet's most effective firepower is concentrated in its air component—about 200 aircraft, most of which are carrier-based. Some reconnaissance and maritime-patrol–antisubmarine aircraft are based ashore, operating from airfields in Spain, Italy, and Greece. The Sixth Fleet's submarine component, much smaller than that of the Soviet Mediterranean Squadron, is employed primarily for antisubmarine warfare.

A NET ASSESSMENT. If military resources were employed with equal skill, the eventual result of combat between U.S. and Soviet forces in and near the Mediterranean would almost certainly be Soviet defeat. Achieving that outcome would cost the United States a great deal. Its losses of ships and aircraft would be high, although such losses could be reduced substantially if the United States were joined in combat by its NATO allies. Still, the fact remains that the USSR has gone to great lengths to establish a position from which it can make the United States pay a price for undertaking military action in and around the Middle East; the United States could not dislodge the USSR from that position without paying the price.

Given this assessment, two questions remain. First, when crises and local conflicts erupt in the region, could the United States continue to provide a reasonable degree of direct support to its allies and friends without first having to fight the USSR? Second, if the USSR must in the process be fought, how long would it take and what forces would be required for the United States (or NATO) to establish the degree of control over the area that the situation called for? In view of the predominant position of the aircraft carrier in the current U.S. military posture in the Mediterranean and of the steps the Soviet Union has taken to prevent the carriers from carrying out their missions, the answers to these two questions depend in large part on assessments of carrier survivability and effectiveness. Could the carriers survive the attacks that the USSR would be likely to launch against them? Could they not only survive but also conduct effective operations?[9]

An honest answer to the question of survivability must be that it

9. Nuclear weapons play no role in this discussion; if they were used, few, if any, warships in the region could be expected to survive.

would depend on a number of factors, many of which are not really knowable in advance: whether the carriers were alerted and prepared for an attack, the strength and tactical character of the attack, the actual performance of offensive and defensive systems, and so forth. How effective the carriers would be if they did survive the attack, however, largely depends on something that is knowable in advance: the numerical strength of the carrier force. Adding carriers to a task force multiplies its overall defensive capability, reduces the impact of losses, and frees a larger proportion of each carrier's air wing for tasks other than the immediate defense of the force. In short, the classic military principle of concentration of forces continues to be valid in conventional naval warfare. Beyond that, little can be said about the effectiveness of the carrier force that is not intimately interwoven with questions of the design capabilities and actual combat performance of sensors, command-control-and-communications systems, and weapons.

Answers to these capability and performance questions can only be estimated, but in the end these estimates will largely determine the answer to the first question: will the United States have to fight in a crisis in the Mediterranean? If the USSR believes itself unable to extract a significant price from the United States in the event of war in the Mediterranean, it is unlikely to press whatever issues might be at stake. But if the price it can force the United States to pay is esti mated by Soviet leaders to be high, deterring Soviet intervention in the Middle East is likely to be more difficult.

MAINTAINING A CREDIBLE U.S. MILITARY POSTURE. Perceptions of relative military capabilities are affected by the statements and styles of political leaders, by national moods engendered by economic trends, by extraneous events such as satellite launches and moon walks, by memories of past wars won or lost, and by countless other factors. This is not to gainsay the importance of the actual physical capacities of the military units—quite the contrary. Perceptions of relative military capabilities may vary within a broad range, but the boundaries of that range are determined—through ill-understood processes—by how, in fact, those relative capabilities would be assessed by an "objective observer." Thus though much can be done to improve (or to damage) perceptions of the U.S. military posture in the Mediterranean through nonmilitary means, in the end it is the actual capabilities of the forces deployed there that count.

Nothing in the Ford administration's defense program, or in the changes made in it by the Carter administration, would have a significant short-term impact on the U.S.-Soviet balance in the Middle East, although options are available that could have immediate and beneficial effects. Some of the steps that are proposed in the 1978 budget should improve the situation, but since all involve the acquisition of new hardware, they would have little bearing until the mid-1980s.

Chief among these long-term improvements is the initiation of programs to acquire, first, aircraft carriers that are sufficiently smaller, and hence cheaper, to be obtainable in larger numbers than would be the case for the present *Nimitz*-class, and second, high-performance combat aircraft that can operate from other than large-deck carriers—i.e., interceptor, attack, and other types of vertical or short takeoff and landing aircraft that can be deployed aboard carriers of any size or on other warships. In addition, acquisition of the AEGIS air defense system should help escort ships protect the carriers from attack. The Carter administration's decision to deploy AEGIS aboard conventional rather than nuclear-powered ships means that more of these systems can be bought and that they should reach operational status sooner. In the same vein, accelerating the installation of towed sonar arrays in both surface combatants and submarines—a step not proposed for fiscal 1978—would increase the Sixth Fleet's ability to detect submarines at very long ranges, in the process providing the carriers with even better protection against surprise.

In the short term, a number of steps are available that would immediately improve the balance in the Middle East. These include modifications in the way existing U.S. forces are used, as well as diplomatic efforts to improve the political-military environment in which U.S. forces deployed in the Middle East must operate.

First, carrier operating patterns could be modified to increase the Navy's capability to surge a truly large force into the Mediterranean or the Indian Ocean *when the situation warrants such a presence there*. This could be accomplished by improving maintenance, manning, and training procedures so as to decrease the "turn-around time" between cruises; modifying the current, essentially rigid pattern of forward deployments, which results in a large fraction of the available force being present in the Mediterranean whether the situation requires its presence there or not, using up whatever slack might otherwise be available for crisis deployments; and shifting from the equally rigid 50-50 split between Atlantic and Pacific that has for decades characterized the disposition of Navy general purpose forces to a more flexible posture so as to increase the number of ships operating in the Atlantic and thus available for deployment to the Mediterranean (and should the situation in the Pacific take an unexpected turn, to augment the forces remaining there).

Second, the activity levels of deployed naval forces—the time ships and aircraft actually spend at sea and in the air—could be increased substantially. At present, the resources allocated to operations provide only "the minimum operational time they need to perform the absolutely necessary combat training."[10] This, however, does not provide the steaming days and flight hours necessary to maintain optimal proficiency. As the gap between U.S. and Soviet naval capabilities continues to narrow, the importance of operational proficiency increases. Furthermore, constraints on operating time often have debilitating collateral effects. Given both the fiscal constraints on operations and the present political situation in the eastern Mediterranean, which has restricted the Sixth Fleet's access to Greek and Turkish ports, not only has the fleet become less active, but it has become something of a fixture at bases in the western Mediterranean. This imposes rather heavily on the hospitality of Spain and Italy, and possibly gives misleading signals to both friends and opponents.

Third, and closely connected with the problem outlined above, is the question what the United States might do to regain access to the military facilities previously provided by Greece and Turkey. The present situation, in which access to local facilities has been curtailed in both nations, is—from a military standpoint, at least—the worst of all possible worlds. If friendly relations with both Greece and Turkey cannot be restored, the United States could decide, in effect, to choose one side or the other. Potential gains must of course be weighed against the costs of further alienating one side in the controversy. Presumably, however, neither would align itself with the Warsaw Pact, and such a decision would permit the return of U.S. forces to bases in the nation that was selected, increasing the freedom of movement of the Sixth Fleet and permitting the U.S. Air Force to deploy a larger number of tactical air squadrons to the eastern Medi-

10. "Annual Defense Department Report, FY 1978," p. 189.

terranean. Ultimately, the benefit would be the reestablishment of a more favorable balance in the eastern Mediterranean, improving the ability of the United States to defend its NATO allies (including Greece and Turkey) and strengthening its influence on the course of events in the Middle East.

The Military Balance in East Asia*

In East Asia, the possibility of direct confrontation with the Soviet Union is more remote than in Europe or the Middle East. The Soviet Union maintains approximately one-fourth of its ground and tactical air forces in the Far East, but they are arrayed primarily against Chinese forces across the border in Manchuria. They do not threaten U.S. interests directly and the likelihood of U.S. forces being drawn into conflict with them is minute. Despite concern about what might happen following Mao's death, there is little, if any, indication of an improvement in Sino-Soviet relations sufficient to free these Soviet military forces for use against NATO.

Direct U.S. military involvement with China is also a remote possibility. China, though its armed forces are immense, has little ability to project military power beyond its borders. Its small nuclear weapons inventory is a threat primarily to the USSR. Since the early 1960s, when China's direct access to Soviet military technology was severed, its forces have been operating with increasingly obsolescent equipment. While the China-Taiwan question remains a possible source of friction for the United States, the adjustment of U.S. relations with those nations is proceeding diplomatically.

The reason for the U.S. military presence in East Asia is not that U.S. interests are directly threatened, but that trends in the Asian military balance might influence the policies of the principal U.S. ally in the region, Japan. That Japan has eschewed the buildup of a strong armed force despite its obvious economic capacity to do so is in part the result of a continuing faith in the U.S. defense commitment, as embodied in the U.S.-Japan Mutual Security Treaty. Japan's policy of maintaining a low military profile, a policy strongly supported by the United States, was reaffirmed in 1976 when Japan ratified the Treaty on the Non-Proliferation of Nuclear Weapons. There are other obstacles to Japan's development of nuclear weapons, not the least of which is adverse domestic opinion. Nevertheless, a nuclear-

---

* This section was prepared by Stuart E. Johnson.

armed Japan is not an inconceivable future development; if it happened, the effects would be unsettling throughout Asia. Since Japan is unlikely to decide to develop nuclear weapons unless it is suddenly imbued with an overriding sense of national insecurity, the U.S. forces that provide visible confirmation of American defense commitments in Northeast Asia have assumed major political significance.

While watching with interest the relative strength of all U.S. armed forces, Japanese leaders take special note of the naval balance in the western Pacific and prospects for stability on the Korean peninsula. An island with meager natural resources, Japan has developed an economy critically dependent on generous imports of raw materials and access to world markets for exports. The flow of petroleum from the Persian Gulf is the most obviously vital sea lane, but the trans-Pacific trade route is also important. Japanese leaders also are concerned about the possibility of violent conflict in nearby Korea. When threats to the security of South Korea are accentuated, as after the fall of the U.S.-backed regime in Vietnam, Japanese officials express greater concern about their own security.

THE THREAT OF A BLOCKADE OF JAPAN. Compared to Soviet naval capabilities elsewhere, the maritime threat in the Pacific is a relatively small one. There has been a relative increase in the Pacific Fleet's strength since 1968, but this reflects the initiation and growth of Soviet naval operations in the Indian Ocean. These deployments are supported by the Pacific Fleet, which has received additional resources to carry out this task. Even so, the Soviet Pacific Fleet remains the weak sister of the four fleets that make up the Soviet Navy.

Arrayed against the Soviet Pacific Fleet are the small but relatively modern Japanese Navy and the more powerful U.S. Seventh Fleet. The latter includes two aircraft carrier task groups, one of which is home-ported at Yokosuka, Japan. The United States also maintains the Third Fleet—including four more carrier task groups—in the eastern Pacific. Many of these ships could move westward fairly rapidly to reinforce the Seventh Fleet if needed. Finally, the United States maintains some land-based antisubmarine and fighter aircraft in the western Pacific, which would be useful in any naval battle that took place there.

The prospects of a blockade of Japan succeeding are related to how long both the Soviet Union and Japan think it could be maintained, and how long the Japanese economy could survive without the normal flow of imports. Petroleum reserves illustrate the magnitude of this question. In the wake of the 1973 oil embargo, Japan set a goal of stockpiling ninety days' supply of petroleum. The stockpiles now contain more than sixty days' worth and are scheduled to reach the objective by 1979. This reserve, coupled with rationing measures, would make a successful blockade of Japan's petroleum shipments a tenuous proposition so long as the Japanese were prepared to resist the coercion. This, in turn, would hinge on Japanese leaders being convinced that they have the support of the United States and that the U.S. and Japanese navies are adequate to defeat the Soviet Navy in the Pacific.

On balance, this task does not seem too difficult. Most of the Soviet Pacific Fleet's operations originate in Vladivostok; ships from this naval complex must pass through one of several straits bounded by Japanese territory before reaching open waters. The straits are choke points that can be mined or blockaded, bottling up Soviet submarines and warships caught inside the Sea of Japan and isolating those already deployed. Without free access to their home port, Soviet combatants previously deployed would not be effective for long. Soviet naval facilities elsewhere, such as those in Somalia, could provide only limited assistance. To circumvent the restricted access from Vladivostok to the open ocean, the USSR has expanded operations at Petropavlovsk on the Kamchatka peninsula, but this has not solved the problem. Petropavlovsk does not have adequate road or rail links with the mainland and must be supplied by ship, a vulnerable link. Without this resupply, it is not clear how long operations from Petropavlovsk could continue.

Thus fewer forces are needed to counter the Soviet Navy in the Pacific than elsewhere; the Soviet Pacific Fleet is less capable and the geography of the region places the Soviet Navy at a distinct disadvantage. In all likelihood, the forces the United States now maintains in the region are larger than required by a realistic assessment of needs. Hence, in military terms, shifting some U.S. naval forces from the Pacific to the Atlantic to help counter the threat to U.S. interests in the Middle East seems sensible. The difficulty would be to do so without implying a lessening of the U.S. commitment to the defense of Japan, particularly in view of the changes being made in U.S. forces in Korea—the second Japanese concern.

THE THREAT IN KOREA. More than two decades after the signing of the armistice in 1953, North Korea and South Korea remain implacable enemies and maintain large, heavily armed forces arrayed against one another. Although all Chinese troops have long since left North Korea, 40,000 American military personnel remain in the South.

In 1971 the U.S. Army's Seventh Infantry Division was removed from Korea, leaving the Second Infantry Division as the last U.S. ground combat force on the peninsula. This withdrawal reflected the general satisfaction of the U.S. and South Korean governments with the military balance. Still, in that same year, the Republic of Korea (ROK), with $1.5 billion assistance from the United States, embarked on a five-year program to upgrade the quality of its armed forces. Today, ROK active ground forces are well armed and total about 560,000 men; they face a North Korean army of 430,000 men. ROK forces have developed significant capabilities against armor— the essence of the threat against them. In addition, the mountainous terrain in Korea means that tank forces would be generally restricted to corridors. Consequently, the amount of armor that the North could usefully employ in battle would be limited and its massed road-bound armor would be vulnerable to attack by air or ground forces. In short, the balance of ground combat forces appears to be adequate; from a strictly military standpoint, the U.S. Second Division contributes only marginally to the South's combat potential. In March 1977 President Carter announced his intention of removing all U.S. ground forces from the peninsula by 1982.

The ROK Air Force, on the other hand, is not adequate for South Korea's needs. The North has about three times as many aircraft as the South. Although ROK aircraft are generally more modern and its pilots are believed to be well trained, South Korea could not rely on its air power surviving against the North. However, the United States maintains a full air wing of F-4D/E tactical fighter aircraft in Korea, sixty-six in all.[11] These units train with ROK units and are prepared to operate jointly with them. Although adding in the U.S. aircraft does not wholly eliminate the North's advantage in numbers, the combined ROK and U.S. air resources represent an overall capability at least comparable to that of North Korea. Moreover, U.S. Air Force and Marine Corps aircraft based in Japan would be available for

11. There are actually two wing headquarters in Korea, but together they include only three combat squadrons—the usual complement of one wing.

rapid reinforcement, as would U.S. Navy aircraft based on carriers. To hedge against a situation in which the *Midway*—the carrier based at Yokosuka—was in port for repairs and thus not available, a support kit enabling the carrier aircraft to operate routinely from land bases would enhance their operational flexibility at modest cost. There is no plan to reduce the U.S. Air Force presence in Korea.

Aircraft alone cannot defend South Korea against air attacks. Since flight times from North Korean air bases near the demilitarized zone are short, interceptor aircraft would have difficulty reacting effectively. Thus additional air defense has been provided by stationing U.S. Nike-Hercules and Hawk surface-to-air missiles in South Korea. The Nike-Hercules missile sites were recently transferred from U.S. to ROK control, but the Hawk missiles are still operated by the U.S. Army. Many are situated to defend communications and surveillance installations and air defense radar sites, which are generally located on high ground and therefore vulnerable to strikes from the air. Plans to train ROK operators of the Hawk have been formulated; the transfer of responsibility for the system is scheduled for 1982.

Another U.S. Army unit in Korea is the Missile Command, which controls nuclear warheads for surface-to-surface missiles. The Army chief of staff, General Bernard Rogers, recently announced that some of these weapons were being withdrawn. The U.S. Air Force also maintains nuclear weapons on the peninsula.

The balance in Korea is likely to continue to favor the South. The ROK government's new five-year Force Improvement Plan will result in the modernization and modest expansion of the ROK Air Force. The North's air force is likely to remain numerically superior, but the ROK Air Force should, upon completion of the plan, be able to put up stiff resistance to air attack and, combined with the USAF air wing, should be sufficient to provide a sure air defense and ground attack capability.

TAILORING U.S. FORCES TO THESE THREATS. Now that the ROK has succeeded in building up a strong conventional defense, it would seem appropriate for the U.S. nuclear weapons remaining in Korea to be removed. Maintaining the weapons in Korea—symbolic of U.S. reliance on nuclear threats—contradicts the emphasis in U.S. policy on curbing the proliferation of nuclear weapons, as well as incurring some risk of seizure or accident. The Carter administration has moved at least partway toward the adoption of such a course by withdrawing some nuclear-capable surface-to-surface missiles; removing the remaining Army and Air Force weapons would also make sense. If a threat from the North seemed imminent and a strong deterrent signal seemed advisable, nuclear weapons could be returned to Korea in short order.

Since the U.S. Second Division contributes only marginally to ROK defenses, the administration's decision to withdraw it and turn over full responsibility for ground combat to South Korea makes sense militarily. U.S. Air Force units will remain in Korea, training and exercising with the ROK Air Force and providing evidence of the U.S. commitment to South Korea's defense. Army air defense units will remain while ROK personnel are trained to operate the Hawk installations, and U.S. personnel that operate sophisticated communications and surveillance systems would remain as well. All told, there might be 12,000 U.S. military personnel in Korea following withdrawal of the division and supporting logistics units.

The favorable ground balance on the Korean peninsula also raises the question whether it is necessary to maintain the Third U.S. Marine Division on Okinawa. The presence of the division causes some difficulties with the local population and, because Marines on this tour of duty are unaccompanied by their families, aggravates recruitment and retention problems for the Corps. The Japanese pay little attention to the Marines as evidence of U.S. commitments. A modest Marine presence in the western Pacific remains desirable for various minor contingencies, but these purposes could be fulfilled by maintaining one or two battalions afloat on amphibious ships in the region and supporting them, in turn, from Hawaii or by a smaller Marine force on Okinawa.

Thus on military grounds alone sizable reductions could be made in the U.S. military presence in East Asia: the ground forces and nuclear weapons could be withdrawn from Korea, many of the Marines could leave Okinawa, and part of the Navy now in the Pacific could be redeployed. Clearly, changes like these—or even more modest ones—should be carried out gradually, leaving ample time for the South Korean and Japanese governments to adjust their own military plannning to the new situation.

Moreover, other steps would have to be taken to ameliorate the political consequences of the withdrawals; to avoid giving the false impression that these reductions implied lessened U.S. commitments in Northeast Asia. Consultations with concerned governments, strong public reaffirmation of commitments, accelerated arms transfers to

South Korea and Japan, and military exercises designed to show the U.S. ability to return to the peninsula in force, should that become necessary, would all be helpful.

In essence, what has happened in East Asia is that a military force posture built for a different time and different political circumstances has acquired a symbolism far beyond its present military relevance, making it difficult to adjust the U.S. military presence in the region to new political realities. But symbols can be changed without adverse consequences if done slowly and carefully. To leave U.S. forces in Asia unchanged would be to foolishly squander substantial resources at a time when the Soviet military buildup makes their potential contribution to the defense of U.S. interests in other regions all the more valuable.

Easing the Burden of Defense*

The degree to which efforts to match, or offset, improvements in Soviet military capabilities increase the financial burden of defense will largely depend on how efficiently U.S. defense resources are managed. Quite apart from changes in force levels, accelerations or slowdowns in weapon modernization programs, and increases or decreases in the operational readiness of military units, the future trend in defense spending will rest on the success or failure of measures to raise the amount of relevant combat potential received for each dollar allocated to defense. In turn, over the past decade, the question of efficiency has been dominated by changes in the cost of manpower.[12]

From 1968 to 1975 manpower costs increased by about 42 percent while the remainder of the defense budget decreased by 7 percent. In effect, spiraling manpower costs required retrenchment in weapon acquisition programs and operations. Since fiscal 1975, however, manpower costs have grown by only 20 percent while the rest of the budget increased by 61 percent. In other words, more effective control of manpower costs made it easier to accelerate the acquisition of weapons, raise the level of operational readiness, and even expand force levels. These contrasting situations are illustrated in table 11.

Three factors caused the sharp increase in manpower costs during

* This section was prepared by Martin Binkin.
12. As used here, manpower costs include the direct cost of military and defense civilian employees, payments to retired military personnel, the costs associated with individual training, medical support, recruitment, and education of overseas dependents, and a portion of base operating costs.

Table 11. Manpower and Other Defense Costs, Fiscal Years 1968, 1975, and 1978
Total obligational authority in billions of dollars

				Percentage increase	
Cost	1968	1975	1978	1968–75	1975–78
Total	75.6	87.8	120.4	16	37
Manpower	36.1	51.2	61.3	42	20
Other	39.5	36.8	59.1	−7	61
Manpower as a percentage of total	48	58	51	...	...

Source: Office of the Assistant Secretary of Defense (Manpower and Reserve Affairs), "Manpower Requirements Report for FY 1978" (March 1977; processed), p. XV-13.

the earlier period. First, the price of manpower rose because of both a jump in federal pay and an upward creep in the average grade of military and civilian employees; second, the cost of military retirement steadily escalated as the number of retirees and the size of their pensions increased; and third, the ratio of support to combat forces rose as the drop in the size of the defense work force did not keep pace with the drop in combat force levels.

In the past several years, steps have been taken to reverse these trends. Growth in the price of defense manpower has been markedly curtailed, the rise in the cost of military retired pay has been partly checked, and there are signs that the armed services are moving toward a more efficient use of defense manpower.

The price of defense manpower has been restrained largely by changes in the methods by which annual pay increases are calculated.[13] First, an anomaly in the formula used to compute annual military pay raises, which had the effect of increasing military pay by more than was necessary to maintain comparability with the private sector—the legal criterion—was corrected in 1974. Second, the proportion of military pay raises allocated to the allowance for quarters, or housing, was increased, thus raising the "rent" paid by military personnel occupying government housing—actually, the amount withheld from their checks for quarters—and thereby reducing the military payroll. Third, the process by which "white-collar" pay was set was adjusted in 1976 by broadening the occupational base of the

13. In addition, to offset inflationary pressures in 1975, the administration imposed a 5 percent limitation on the cost-of-living raise in federal salaries (military and civilian). The purpose of this "pay cap" was said to be to "set an example for the rest of the economy." See *The Budget of the United States Government, Fiscal Year 1976*, pp. 7–8. Perhaps incidentally, this pay cap also compensated for previous cost-of-living raises that seemed to exceed the rate of inflation.

Table 12. Average Annual Percentage Increases in Pay of Defense Employees and in the Consumer Price Index, Fiscal Years 1968-75 and 1975-78

Description	1968–75	1975–78
Composite defense payroll	**9.0**	**6.4**
Military pay	10.5	5.8
Civilian pay	8.1	7.7
Classified (white-collar)	6.9	6.0
Wage board (blue-collar)	8.2	9.7
Military retirement pay	**8.5**	**7.7**
Consumer price index	**6.2**	**6.3**

Source: Author's estimates derived from data appearing in Office of the Assistant Secretary of Defense (Comptroller), "National Defense Budget Estimates for FY 1978" (1977; processed), p. 123.

annual comparability survey and adopting more statistically sound methods of applying the survey data. Finally, the "1 percent kicker," the 1 percent added to cost-of-living increases which overcompensated for the delay between a rise in prices and the retiree's receipt of a larger annuity, was eliminated from retired pay adjustments. Though each change was seemingly minor, the financial implications have been marked. Because of these changes, fiscal 1978 manpower costs are at least $4 billion, about 6 percent, below what they otherwise would have been. Over time, the savings will grow larger.

As a result, the average annual rate of increase in the defense payroll slowed from 9.0 percent during the fiscal 1968–75 period to 6.4 percent during the past three years (table 12). The sharpest reduction occurred in military pay; indeed, since 1975 military pay increases have not kept pace with the cost of living. White-collar civilian employees fared slightly better, but their pay also failed to match increases in the consumer price index. On the other hand, although the average annual rate of increase in military retired pay declined, it remained higher than the rate of inflation. Blue-collar defense workers did even better. Since 1975 their annual pay raises, calculated by a unique method, have increased at an even faster rate than in the earlier period. Legislation to reform the federal wage system for blue-collar employees, proposed in 1976 but not passed by Congress, has been resubmitted.[14]

14. As matters now stand, many blue-collar defense employees are better paid than their counterparts in private industry. Three changes have been proposed to correct this situation. The first would match the average federal wage to the average local prevailing wage, instead of using the present system in which step 2 of the federal wage scale is matched to the local wage. Since most federal workers are paid

Table 13. Average Annual Percentage Changes in Per Capita Pay Attributable
to Changes in Grade Structure, Fiscal Years 1968–75 and 1975–78[a]

Classification	1968–75	1975–78
Military personnel	1.14	−1.00
Civilian personnel		
Classified (white-collar)	0.63	1.11
Wage board (blue-collar)	0.19	0.28

Source: Author's estimates derived from unpublished data provided by the Office of the Assistant Secretary of Defense (Comptroller), March 1977.

a. Strictly speaking, some of the variation in per capita pay can be attributed to factors other than changes in the grade structure, such as differences in the amount of civilian overtime pay. Because the overall effect of these other factors is relatively small, it has been ignored.

Changes in grade distribution also affected the average pay of military and civilian employees. On the military side, the upward creep in the grade structure, characteristic of the 1968–75 period, has been reversed in the past three years, bringing significant savings. On the civilian side, the upward pressure on the white-collar grade structure, which was most evident in the 1968–72 period, has accelerated once again after stabilizing between fiscal years 1973 and 1975. These changes are summarized in table 13. To illustrate the financial implications, consider that if the grade distribution that existed in fiscal 1975 prevailed in fiscal 1978, the 1978 military pay bill would be close to $600 million greater, the white-collar payroll would be about $350 million lower, and the blue-collar payroll some $50 million lower.

Steps also have been taken to improve the efficiency with which defense manpower is used, but results are difficult to measure. One way to quantify the gains is to estimate manpower costs (in constant dollars) associated with each unit of output of the armed forces and compare the results for different years. This highly aggregated measure is shown in table 14.

Conclusions about the gains traceable to greater manpower efficiency depend largely on the measure of output used. This is most apparent for the Navy, which now spends close to 65 percent more for manpower per ship than it did in fiscal 1964. When adjustments are made to account for increases in technology, complexity, and capabil-

at steps 4 or 5, they often receive up to 12 percent more than the local average. Second, the Monroney Amendment, which bases wage rates in some small communities on higher rates "imported" from large urban areas, would be repealed. Finally, the uniform night shift differential pay rate would be replaced by locally established differentials.

Table 14. Changes in Manpower Costs and in Various Measures of Military Output, Fiscal Years 1964 and 1978

Description	1964	1978	Percentage change, 1964–78
Army			
Manpower costs (billions of 1978 dollars)[a]	20.5	18.4	−10
Active and reserve maneuver battalions	368	373	1
Active and reserve armored division equivalents[b]	21.3	26.9	26
Navy[c]			
Manpower costs (billions of 1978 dollars)[a]	15.7	13.1	−17
Ships (number)	917	464	−49
Standard displacement (millions of tons)	7.6	5.3	−30
Shaft horsepower (millions)	26.6	18.2	−32
Electrical generating capacity (megawatts)	1.9	2.0	5
Air Force			
Manpower costs (billions of 1978 dollars)[a]	20.4	13.9	−32
Strategic forces			
Total number of aircraft and missiles[d]	2,782	1,955	−30
Missile throw-weight (millions of pounds)[e]	2.1	2.2	5
Bomber payload (millions of pounds)[f]	49.8	23.8	−52
Air defense forces			
Number of aircraft	1,543	321	−79
Total aircraft weight (millions of tons)	44.1	11.9	−73
Tactical air forces			
Number of aircraft	2,624	2,400	−9
Offensive load-carrying capacity (millions of ton-miles)[g]	5.8	13.3	129
Airlift forces			
Number of aircraft	2,243	1,078	−52
Total lift (millions of ton-miles)[h]	18.5	42.3	129

Sources: Army output measures based on data appearing in Department of Defense, "A Report to Congress on U.S. Conventional Reinforcements for NATO" (June 1976; processed). Navy measures based on unpublished data provided by the Department of the Navy, March 1977. Air Force figures derived from data appearing in IISS, *The Military Balance, 1964–1965* and *1976–77;* Strategic Air Command, "The Development of the Strategic Air Command, 1946–1976" (March 21, 1976; processed), pp. 113–18; *Department of Defense Appropriations for Fiscal Year 1978,* Hearings before the House Appropriations Committee, 95:1, pt. 1 (GPO, 1977), pp. 474–569; Department of Defense, "Department of Defense Manpower, FY 64–FY 77: The Components of Change" (April 1975; processed), pp. 19, 24, 25. Manpower costs based on data provided by the Office of the Assistant Secretary of Defense (Comptroller), March 1977.

a. Constant-dollar figures tell us how much the personnel on duty in 1964 would have cost if 1978 pay rates had then obtained, providing a realistic comparison of the level of resources devoted to defense manpower. In these terms, the Army will spend about 10 percent less on manpower in fiscal 1978 than it spent in fiscal 1964.

b. An armored division equivalent is a measure of overall combat capability that takes into account both the quality and quantity of weapons composing a land force. It is based on the on-hand capabilities of a U.S. armored division operating on terrain such as would be encountered in Europe. It does not take into account sustaining capabilities, such as ammunition and fuel stocks.

c. Excludes strategic submarines.

d. Includes strategic bombers, tanker aircraft, and ICBMs.

e. Ballistic missile throw-weight is the maximum useful weight that has been tested on the boost stages of the missile. It includes the weight of the reentry vehicles, penetration aids, dispensing and release

ity, however, a different picture emerges. For example, if the size of ships or their engines' power is taken into account and manpower costs are counted per displacement ton or shaft horsepower, the loss of manpower efficiency is less marked. If electrical generating capacity—a proxy for technological sophistication—is used as an output measure, the Navy is using manpower less intensively (more efficiently) than it did in 1964.

Similar conclusions apply to the use of Air Force manpower. Manpower cost per major weapon platform (aircraft or missiles) has gone up substantially since 1964. When adjustments are made to account for improvements in capability, however, different results are obtained. Most notable have been improvements in the tactical and airlift forces, where manpower costs per unit of capability have been cut dramatically.

Reductions in Army manpower costs are evident by almost any measure. Manpower cost per maneuver battalion is about 12 percent lower than in 1964; after adjusting for improvements in capability, manpower cost per unit (armored division equivalent) is about 30 percent lower than in 1964.

Caution must be exercised in interpreting these results, since the data do not include the cost of contracted services. While there are signs that the services are relying on contract support to an increasing extent, the magnitude of the shift is unknown. To the extent that this is true, actual manpower costs per unit of output would be greater than those shown in table 14.

In any case, much greater manpower savings are possible. The savings that would be realized from the legislation to rectify the upward bias in present methods for calculating raises in the pay of blue-collar employees would amount to $200 million in fiscal 1978 and grow to $700 million a year within five years. Also, early attention to controlling the continuing growth in the average grade of white-collar civilians could produce large savings; as noted, merely returning to the grade distribution that prevailed in fiscal 1974 would save $350 million at fiscal 1978 prices. Defense manpower could also be used more efficiently if measures discussed in various editions of

---

mechanisms, reentry shrouds, covers, buses, and propulsion devices with their propellants, all of which are still present at the end of the boost phase.

f. Bomber payload is the maximum weight of ordnance that an aircraft can carry.

g. The product of combat radius and payload, summed over all tactical aircraft in the inventory.

h. The product of combat radius and lift capacity per day, summed over all airlift aircraft.

the annual Brookings publication, *Setting National Priorities,* were put into effect: the length of military training courses could be shortened, more people could be trained on the job instead of in classrooms, and tours of duty could be lengthened.

High on the list of possible reforms are changes in the military retirement system. The Carter administration has announced that it plans to establish a blue-ribbon panel to examine the military compensation system, including its retirement provisions. If these provisions were simply aligned with those governing federal civilian retirement, savings would be substantial over the long term.

Emerging problems surrounding the all-volunteer forces may make the quest for manpower savings more difficult. Two disquieting factors on the horizon are the imminent decline in the number of young men in the population as the postwar baby boom runs its course and the diminishing proportion likely to volunteer as the economy improves. Both factors will make military recruitment more difficult.

A few years from now, as the effects of dwindling birthrates in the 1960s begin to be felt, the number of young men reaching the age of eighteen each year will decline sharply from present levels, dropping 15 percent by 1985 and over 25 percent by 1992. If the armed forces remain at their present size, recruiting will be more difficult; instead of having to attract one of every six males, as is now the case, the military services eventually will have to attract one of every four. Moreover, assuming that the economy continues to recover, the number of male high school graduates attracted to military service could become disturbingly small and require an increase in military pay relative to civilian pay in order to meet recruitment needs. If this is not done, if military pay raises only match civilian pay raises, by 1981 the services will be fortunate to attract 80 percent of their stated needs for high school graduates; by 1985 that figure is likely to decrease to 63 percent. The greater the economic recovery, of course, the greater the shortfall.

As it becomes harder for the military services to meet their quantitative or qualitative goals, pressure will mount to solve these problems by returning to conscription, by reducing military strength levels, or by further increasing military pay. But there are other ways to overcome these difficulties, should they develop, or better still to avert them altogether.

For example, the armed forces could effectively use more women and civilians, thereby reducing the demand for male volunteers and alleviating the recruiting problem.[15] Moreover, partly because of excessively liberal discharge policies, volunteers are leaving the services before they complete their first enlistment at almost twice the rate that prevailed before the draft was abolished. Through tighter management and more careful recruitment, the average length of enlistment could be increased, personnel turnover would decrease, and fewer recruits would be needed each year.

It may also be the case that current educational, aptitude, and physical standards are higher than necessary, or simply inappropriate for the satisfactory performance of many military duties. Relatively minor adjustments in these standards could yield substantial increases in the supply of qualified males. For example, simply extending maximum and minimum weight limits by 10 percent would increase the supply of eligible recruits by 5 percent. Returning to the more lenient educational and aptitude standards of 1974 would reduce the need for highly qualified males by close to 15 percent.[16]

Finally, this situation makes it all the more important to ensure that military personnel are fully aware of the value of their compensation. The compensation system used today, which is geared to meet the needs of the military establishment of an earlier era, is out of date. Those already in the armed services, prospective volunteers, and lawmakers are often unaware of the full value of military compensation simply because some of its elements are received in kind or as part of a confusing system of special allowances and tax benefits. Moreover, because its underlying rationale calls for paying people on the basis of their "needs" rather than strictly for their contribution to national security, the compensation system in some instances attracts those who are costly in relation to their skills. As a result, the United States is paying more than is necessary to field its present military forces. Many of these problems could be resolved by paying the military in much the same fashion as civilians are paid. The present hodgepodge of military pay, allowances, and tax benefits would give way to the payment of a single "salary." Earnings would become

15. See Martin Binkin and Shirley J. Bach, *Women and the Military* (Brookings Institution, 1977).

16. Congressional Budget Office, *The Costs of Defense Manpower: Issues for 1977* (GPO, 1977), pp. 52–53.

more apparent, more understandable, and hence easier for everyone to evaluate.

Because such proposals call for changes in defense manpower management, they are unpopular among military traditionalists. Yet the risks of adopting these options to make the all-volunteer system work would be small compared to the social and political costs of renewing conscription, the financial cost of increasing incentives, or the military cost of reducing strength levels.

Reversing the Trend in Defense Spending

With each passing year it has become more difficult to explain the continuing momentum in the Soviet defense buildup.

At first it seemed likely that the buildup was a reaction of the new Soviet leadership to Nikita Khrushchev's foreign policy reverses from about 1957 through 1962. At the time Soviet armed forces were being cut back drastically, Khrushchev pursued an aggressive foreign policy, more aggressive than could be supported with the military power then available to the USSR. Partly as a result, the Soviet Union suffered a string of political setbacks: in Central Europe, in the Congo, in Cuba, and elsewhere. Moreover, fears stemming from this aggressive stance plus coincident Soviet technological breakthroughs spurred a major rebuilding of U.S. military capabilities during the Kennedy years. This disastrous Soviet foreign policy was no doubt a major factor leading to Khrushchev's overthrow in 1964. And determined to avoid a similar fate, his successors accelerated Soviet defense programs to catch up with the United States.

By the end of the 1960s, however, and certainly by 1972, when a special Soviet position in Eastern Europe and parity in strategic arms had been ratified in formal agreements, it seemed logical that this military buildup would slow down. The Soviet economy (and Soviet consumers) would certainly have benefited from a reduction in the 12 to 15 percent share of Soviet resources consumed by its defense establishment. But there is no evidence of such a reallocation.

Explanations come readily to mind, ranging from the difficulty of turning off bureaucracies once they have been turned on, to speculations that the Soviet military received a promise of continuing high budgetary allocations in exchange for their cooperation on a policy of political rapprochement with the West, to ruminations on the nature of the Russian character as shaped by the searing experience of World War II, to fears that the USSR is indeed seeking military superiority to enable it to coerce, and eventually to dominate, the West. Each of these reasons could have something to do with the continuing buildup. In any case, it seems clear that, as in the late 1950s, the Soviet Union has again underestimated the West, failing to foresee the degree to which its apparent gains would cause the West to become apprehensive and step up its own military preparations. But this is exactly what has happened in the United States since 1975.

The assessments in earlier sections of this monograph demonstrate the value of detailed analyses of the Soviet military buildup. An across-the-board U.S. response stemming from a diffuse sense of unease would only waste resources, diverting people and money not only from important domestic needs, but also, within the armed forces, from those areas where the Soviet Union presents more significant challenges. In East Asia, the Soviet buildup threatens not the United States, but China. Given improvements in U.S.-China relations and more narrow U.S. definitions of its interests in Southeast Asia, the U.S. force posture in the Pacfic could be scaled down, freeing resources for use elsewhere. In the realm of the strategic nuclear competition, both Soviet capabilities and the political consequences of those capabilities are frequently exaggerated. Although some improvements in the U.S. strategic force posture are warranted, a massive response seems inefficient and in some ways counterproductive. In Europe and the Middle East, improving Soviet military capabilities do threaten important U.S. interests and require a clear and strong response. But even here, there are more and less efficient ways of enhancing U.S. military capabilities; concern about trends in the military balance should not cause the neglect of rigorous examinations of proposals on the pragmatic grounds of relative costs and relative effectiveness. Finally, putting into effect the many possible ways of reducing manpower requirements and the growth in military and civilian pay rates would curtail increases in the defense budget resulting from assessed needs to counter the USSR or would at least avoid unexpected increases brought on by inadequate recruitment in the all-volunteer force.

Unfortunately, such an approach has its political difficulties. Sophisticated evaluations of alternative weapon systems and force structures are not persuasive to Congress or the public. Apparently a broad and undifferentiated response is more appealing. The public has stated clearly—in opinion polls, in letters to congressmen, and in its votes during the past year's elections—that it wants the nation's leaders "to do something about the Russians." That is why proposals to improve U.S. military capabilities now receive a sympathetic hearing on Capitol Hill.

If this continues, the U.S. defense budget will increase over the next several years, quite aside from the effects of inflation. In short, 1975 was the year that the arms competition between the United States and the USSR moved forward another ratchet. The Soviet buildup has resulted in a new U.S. buildup, and the competition continues at a higher level. Reversing this trend will require recognition by both nations of its self-defeating nature—recognition that in view of modern military technology and the present nature of the international system, greater expenditures on arms do not necessarily increase security. Indeed, by destabilizing political relations, they may well undermine it.

With such common recognition, arms control negotiations could begin to yield significant results. Although these results would, most importantly, reduce the risk of war and promote greater political and economic cooperation between the superpowers, of particular interest to readers of this book are their potential budgetary effects.

Strategic Arms Limitation

The crucial negotiation is SALT. Although nuclear weapons account for a relatively small share of the two nations' defense budgets, they are the only weapons that significantly threaten the territory and population of both sides. Consequently, their control has implications for broader political relations and for the success or failure of other arms control efforts.

The immediate problem is that the 1972 Interim Agreement to limit strategic offensive weapons expires in October 1977. Should a follow-on agreement not be concluded before then, there would be significant pressure on both sides to step up modernization programs and perhaps to increase strategic force levels. Eventually, if the strategic competition accelerated, pressure to abrogate the 1972 Treaty Limiting the Deployment of Anti-Ballistic Missiles could grow. The budgetary implications of any of these contingencies would be sizable. U.S. officials have mentioned $2 billion to $5 billion as the annual incremental expenditures that would be necessary if the Interim Agreement were to expire without replacement. Building an ABM system would add, at a minimum, another $5 billion annually. And of course the political implications of either development would be grave.

It seems likely that any new agreement would have to follow the guidelines worked out by President Ford and General Secretary Brezhnev at Vladivostok in 1974. The time remaining is probably too short to negotiate a new type of arrangement, and unlike Mr. Carter, Mr. Brezhnev has a vested interest in seeing the labors of 1974 consummated. The Vladivostok accord limits each side to 2,400 strategic missile launchers and heavy bombers, of which 1,320 missiles may carry MIRVs. Adhering to those levels would require no reductions in planned U.S. forces and only minor reductions in present Soviet forces. The few controls on the characteristics of strategic weapons included in the accord would have little impact on modernization programs in either nation. Adding constraints on deployments of cruise missiles and Backfire bombers, a possibility often noted, would still have only minor budgetary impact. In fact, constraints on cruise missiles might lead to higher budgets, in that they would reopen arguments for buying a large number of B-1 bombers.

Thus, it would be left to SALT III, the negotiations following implementation of the Vladivostok accord, to produce an agreement that might also lead to reductions in strategic budgets. Agreement, for example, to reduce each side's total strategic force levels to 1,320 would bring about savings in operating costs and would permit a reduction in the pace of weapon modernization. For the United States, such reductions could mean annual savings of between $800 million and $3.5 billion at 1978 prices from the level of strategic budgets likely without such agreement.[17] The range is wide because potential savings would depend on which existing forces were cut and which were retained. Phasing out bombers, which are more costly to acquire and operate than ICBMs, would yield much greater savings. In any

17. The calculations leading to the low end of the savings range assume that present modernization programs (bombers, Trident submarine, and M-X ICBM) would not be affected by the agreement until the late 1980s. They further assume that only ICBMs would be phased out of the force structure to reach the lower ceiling. Under this assumption, the U.S. force would consist of 656 SLBMs, about 400 bombers, and 250 ICBMs. The calculations leading to the high end of the savings range assume that the M-X program would be sharply curtailed and that bomber force levels would be reduced to about 150.

event, savings are hypothetical; whether they materialized would depend on the effect of the agreement on defense policy in general. If little else changed, reductions in strategic spending could be used for other types of military forces. On the other hand, successful negotiations to cut back strategic force levels so sharply could produce a political atmosphere conducive to unilateral restraint.

Stabilizing the Balance in Europe*

A second negotiating forum of considerable political importance and some potential budgetary consequence is the Vienna talks on mutual and balanced force reductions in Europe. Member states of NATO and the Warsaw Pact have been engaged in these negotiations since October 1973. Although it is encouraging that they have stuck to it for this long, progress to date has been disappointing, basically because the proposals advanced by each side thus far are incompatible.

The Warsaw Pact seeks to preserve roughly the existing balance of forces between East and West, as well as the current balance among members of each alliance. Its proposals thus specify equal reductions, or equal percentage reductions, in manpower for Warsaw Pact and NATO forces in Central Europe, and call for separate ceilings to be placed on the force levels of each country. One proposal, put forth in February 1975, was to simply freeze all forces at existing levels.

NATO argues that the existing East-West balance of forces is unacceptable, and has insisted on a common collective ceiling on ground forces within the agreed geographical area. The last major NATO proposal, made in December 1975, called for a preliminary reduction of 68,000 Soviet ground troops and 1,700 tanks in exchange for U.S. reductions of 29,000 troops, 1,000 nuclear warheads, and 90 nuclear delivery systems—all followed by a second phase reduction to the common collective ceiling of 700,000 ground troops.

Obviously, no agreement can be reached as long as each side remains committed to these positions. Reaching an agreement on asymmetrical reductions—NATO's preference—will be difficult. With no urgent need for Soviet manpower elsewhere, there would seem to be no reason for the Soviet Union to negotiate away its current numerical advantage in Europe. The idea of substituting the withdrawal of some U.S. tactical nuclear weapons for the withdrawal

---

* This section was prepared by Frederick W. Young.

of NATO ground forces has not been categorically rejected, but the USSR is not likely to find such proposals attractive since nuclear weapons could always be quickly returned to Europe by air. Moreover, the Western European members of NATO would oppose any substantial reduction in U.S. nuclear forces, as they fear it would indicate a weakening of the U.S. nuclear commitment.

The Warsaw Pact position calling for ceilings on the forces of individual countries is probably driven by Soviet fear of resurgent German militarism and Soviet desire to maintain control and influence in Eastern Europe. From this point of view, the highest priority would be to obtain a ceiling on West German forces, although the Soviet Union might conceivably see real, if unstated, advantages in an agreement that restricted the size of Eastern European forces as well. Moreover, the USSR may well view U.S. forces in Europe as a stabilizing influence on West Germany. Ceilings placed on each country would make it impossible to substitute German for U.S. troops; either the United States would remain in Europe or there would be a corresponding loss of NATO capability. Analogously, this reasoning would provide a continuing rationale for Soviet forces to remain in Eastern Europe.

Together, these differences over the principles to guide reductions will make attainment of an agreement difficult. Although compromises are certainly possible, it is essential to explore alternative approaches to stability in Europe; for example, the negotiations in Vienna might be used to ease fears of surprise attack.[18] Such measures might involve the location of observers from an international organization at military installations on both sides, a limit on the size of maneuvers, or restrictions on troop rotation procedures. Under present procedures, for example, the USSR could temporarily increase its manpower in Central Europe by some 100,000 troops, enough to mask the buildup for an attack. Indeed, any measure that would significantly increase the warning time before an attack would do more than mutual force reductions to stabilize the military situation in Central Europe. Force reductions degrade the capabilities of both defender and attacker. Steps to increase warning time would differentially weaken the capabilities of any would-be attacker.

18. This suggestion was made by Representative Les Aspin; see *Congressional Record,* daily edition, vol. 123 (February 7, 1977), p. H 911–14. Certain provisions of the 1975 CSCE Agreement, known as confidence-building measures, are steps in this direction.

How the Soviet Union would respond to proposals designed to preclude surprise attacks is unknown. It would see little military advantage in such an agreement since NATO's ability to mount a surprise attack is at best limited. On the other hand, if such proposals were to improve the political situation in Europe without causing a reduction in its forces in Eastern Europe, the Soviet Union might find them worth exploring. By reducing fears of surprise attack, such an agreement would alleviate the principal concern now underlying the U.S. buildup of its NATO forces, and thereby ease pressures on the defense budget. Over the longer term, an improvement in the political atmosphere might result from the agreement and lead to follow-on agreements to reduce force levels.

Naval Arms Control

A third area for arms control with potential budgetary implications concerns the Navy. Here, too, savings are likely to be small, except over a long period. The most promising possibility would be an agreement by the United States and the USSR to limit naval deployments and abolish military facilities in the Indian Ocean region. Soviet spokesmen have mentioned such an agreement favorably, as has President Carter; negotiations are under way.

Again, the savings are hypothetical. They would be realized only if the forces each side now maintains in the region—and the necessary backup forces—were phased out of their respective force structures. Such a reduction would also permit a slight slowdown in shipbuilding programs, with imputed additional savings. For the Soviet Union, for example, the annual potential value of such an agreement might exceed $500 million.[19]

In all probability, however, neither the United States nor the Soviet Union would be willing to reduce its naval forces directly following such an agreement; and anyway each sees a need for larger naval

19. The USSR typically maintains sixteen to twenty ships in the Indian Ocean, operating from bases at Vladivostok and Petropavlovsk. A rough rule of thumb for the U.S. Navy is that it requires three ships in a naval inventory to keep one ship continuously on station in a distant region. According to this rule, the total cost of the roughly fifty to sixty ships necessary to maintain the Soviet Indian Ocean squadron would be at least $6 billion (at U.S. prices). Assuming a twenty-year ship lifetime, an Indian Ocean demilitarization agreement may be said to represent potential annual shipbuilding savings for the USSR of at least $300 million. Operating costs of the squadron are more difficult to estimate, but they would probably amount to another $200 million at U.S. prices.

deployments elsewhere. Still, over the long term, even a limited naval agreement that functioned effectively could reduce requirements for naval forces below the levels that might otherwise obtain. And again, there is the hope that such an agreement could contribute to an improved political atmosphere and lead to other agreements to control naval forces.

Prospects

Paradoxically, the strong U.S. reaction since fiscal 1975 to the Soviet military buildup may have increased the possibilities for successful arms control negotiations. These possibilities are at best tenuous and the negotiations themselves are almost certain to be time consuming and arduous. Nonetheless, a situation in which both East and West are intent on strengthening their military capabilities may also be one in which both sides will most clearly see advantages in negotiating mutual arms restraints.

Successful negotiations of course would do much more than save money. Their primary purposes are to build mutual confidence and reduce suspicion, thereby promoting political cooperation and lessening the risk of war.

Achieving these important objectives, however, will require resolution of the dilemma inherent in present U.S. defense budget planning. In effect, the possibilities for reduced spending in the future may depend on a resolve to continue to spend heavily in the present. Such resolve may be difficult to sustain during the next few years, which are sure to be characterized by sharp competition for budgetary resources and pressure to achieve a balanced budget. This puts a premium on measures to achieve greater efficiency in defense management and on identifying planning criteria that can be used to distinguish between essential, marginal, and whimsical needs for weapons and forces.

In the present international system, the ultimate arbiter remains power; economic and political power most often, but not infrequently military power. In all probability, the Soviet Union can be induced to reach a mutually beneficial accommodation with the West only if it becomes convinced that the United States is willing to take the decisions necessary to compete for this power effectively over the long haul.